Mythological Creatures and the Chinese Zodiac in Origami

Other books by John Montroll:

Origami Sculptures

Prehistoric Origami *Dinosaurs and Other Creatures*

Origami Sea Life by John Montroll and Robert J. Lang

African Animals in Origami

Origami Inside-Out

North American Animals in Origami

Teach Yourself Origami

Bringing Origami to Life

Dollar Bill Animals in Origami

Bugs and Birds in Origami

A Plethora of Polyhedra in Origami

Animal Origami for the Enthusiast

Origami for the Enthusiast

Easy Origami

Birds in Origami

Favorite Animals in Origami

Mythological Creatures
and the Chinese Zodiac
in Origami

John Montroll

Dover Publications, Inc.
New York

To Cindy, Phil, Jonathan, and Adina

Published in Canada by General Publishing Company, Ltd., 30 Lesmill Road, Don Mills, Toronto, Ontario.
Published in the United Kingdom by Constable and Company, Ltd., 3 The Lanchesters, 162–164 Fulham Palace Road, London W6 9ER.

This work is first published in 1996 in separate editions by Antroll Publishing Company, Maryland, and Dover Publications, Inc., New York.

Manufactured in the United States of America
Dover Publications, Inc., 31 East 2nd Street, Mineola, N.Y. 11501

Library of Congress Cataloging-in-Publication Data

Montroll, John.
    Mythological creatures and the Chinese zodiac in origami / John Montroll.
        p.   cm.
    ISBN 0-486-28971-0 (pbk.)
    1. Origami.   2. Animals, Mythical, in art.   3. Zodiac in art.
4. Astrology, Chinese, in art.   I. Title.
TT870.M556   1996
736'.982—dc20
                                            96-2231
                                            CIP

Introduction

*T*his collection of origami projects takes us into the realm of mythology, represented by creatures from both Eastern and Western folklore. You will meet the twelve animals of the Chinese Zodiac, then find yourself in the world of dragons and unicorns.

There are projects for both new and advanced folders, from the simpler diamond, heart, spade, and club to the very complex three-headed dragon. In between you will find a rat, rabbit, horse, monkey, unicorn, and Pegasus to name a few. In the contents the level of difficulty is represented by one, two, three, or four stars.

There are Japanese and Chinese characters for each of the Chinese Zodiac animals. These were skillfully and beautifully drawn by Toshio Mori, the grandfather of my friend Masatsugu Tsutsumi from Japan. There are two kanji characters for each animal. The top one represents the modern character for the animal, the bottom is the ancient character used for the "Year of the (animal)". The Chinese Pinyin pronounciation is given with tonal marks. The Japanese pronounciation is given along with the hiragana (Japanese syllables).

As in all my books, the illustrations conform to the internationally accepted Randlett-Yoshizawa conventions. The colored side of origami paper is represented by the shadings in the diagrams. Origami paper can be found in many hobby shops or purchased by mail from Origami USA, 15 West 77th Street, New York, NY 10024-5192 or from Dover Publications, Inc., 31 East 2nd Street, Mineola, NY 11501. Large sheets are easier to use than small ones.

Many people helped make this book possible. I am grateful to Toshio Mori for the beautifully drawn kanji. Thanks to Marc Hohman and Sean Brenner of St. Anselm's Abbey School in Washington, D.C. for the description of each creature and other text. Thanks to Mary Beth O'Quinn, David Keeler, and niece Rachel Korr for their artistic contribution. Thanks to Joyce Keeler for the Chinese pronounciation. I wish to thank Steve Rollin, Matt Slayton, Michael LaFosse, and Robert Lang for their creative input and support throughout the writing of this book. I would also like to thank my brother Charley for his work as editor. Of course I also thank the many folders who proof-read the diagrams.

John Montroll

Contents

★ Simple
★★ Intermediate
★★★ Complex
★★★★ Very Complex

The Chinese Zodiac

Rat
★★
page 22

Ox
★★★
page 25

Tiger
★★
page 30

Boar
★★★
page 64

Suits

Diamond
★
page 10

Heart
★
page 12

Rabbit
★★
page 33

Dog
★★
page 61

Spade
★
page 14

Club
★★
page 17

Chinese Dragon
★★★
page 36

Rooster
★★★
page 57

Snake
★★
page 41

Monkey
★★★
page 52

Ram
★★
page 49

Horse
★★
page 44

Mythological Creatures

Sea Serpent
★★
page 70

Unicorn
★★★
page 74

Centaur
★★★
page 77

Wyvern
★★★
page 93

Griffin
★★★
page 81

Three-Headed Dragon
★★★★
page 111

Western Dragon
★★★
page 98

Pegasus
★★★
page 85

Chimera
★★★★
page 104

Cerberus
★★★
page 89

Symbols

Lines

– – – – – – – – – –   Valley fold, fold in front.

– · – · – · – · – ·   Mountain fold, fold behind.

——————   Crease line.

············   X-ray or guide line.

Arrows

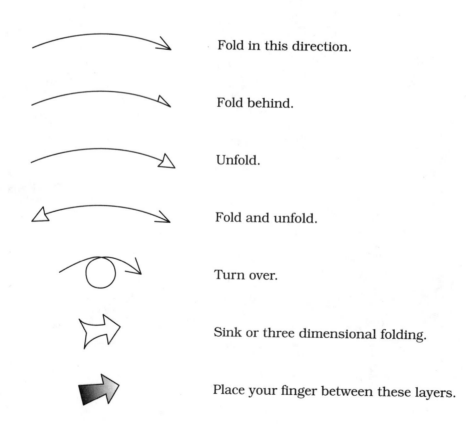

Fold in this direction.

Fold behind.

Unfold.

Fold and unfold.

Turn over.

Sink or three dimensional folding.

Place your finger between these layers.

Dragons inside
Please beware
Enter only
If you dare

Diamond

Playing Cards and Card Suits

The origin of playing cards is largely unknown. The first record of playing cards is from the Orient in the 12th century. Some theorists contend that both cards and chess evolved from a game played with pebbles by shepherds of western Asia. Other theorists believe that playing cards evolve from Egyptian divining rods or arrows that were used for conjuring and divination. Communication with the gods was obtained by casting the rods, marked with four different symbols, upon a central alter; the priests interpreted the commands of the gods according to the direction in which the rod fell. Whatever the origin of playing cards (Oriental, Arabic, or Egyptian), they found their way into European countries in the 12th century, perhaps carried there by traveling merchants, professional soldiers, or wandering tribes of Gypsies.

The diamond symbol is known as a square ("carreau") in French, a bell ("Schelle") in German, and money ("denaro") in Italian.

The card suits evolved through use of different forms and numbers. Early Chinese cards contained suits based on coins. An old Oriental circular pack contained 10 suits of 12 cards each, emblematic of the ten incarnations of the Hindu deity Vishnu. The suits included were represented by figures such as fish, lions, hogs, tortoises, serpents, dwarfs, apes, dragons, shells, men-horse, and wild boars. Early Italian tarot cards contained four emblems (swords, cups, rings, and batons) which were the emblems held in the four hands of the two-headed Indian deity Ardhanari. French cardmakers created the current designs of suit symbols and devised the two-color system for easy identification. Early court cards (Kings, Queens, and Jacks) portrayed various European rulers, but these cards were standardized into their current form by the early 19th century.

1

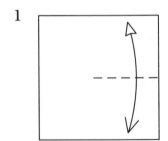

Fold and unfold creasing only on the right side.

2

Fold the corner to the center line.

3

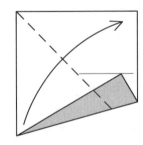

Fold one corner to the opposite corner.

4

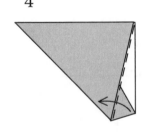

5

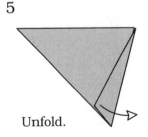

Unfold.

6

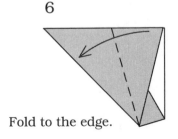

Fold to the edge.

7

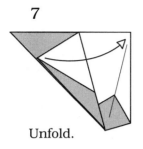

Unfold.

8

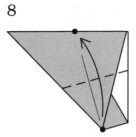

Fold up from dot to dot.

9

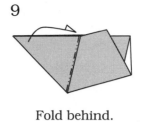

Fold behind.

10

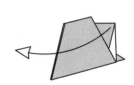

Unfold almost everything.

11

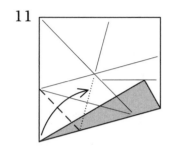

Fold along the dotted line.

12

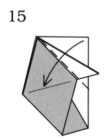

Pull out to the edge.

13

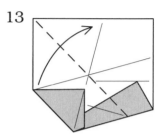

Fold along the crease.

14

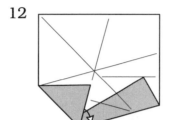

Reverse-fold along the crease.

15

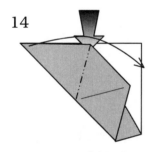

Fold the layers together.

16

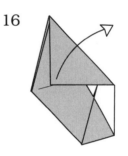

Unfold.

17

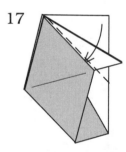

Fold underneath.

18

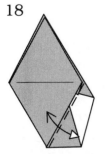

Fold and unfold.

19

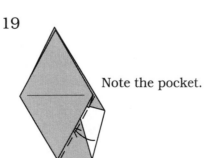

Note the pocket.

Tuck inside.

20

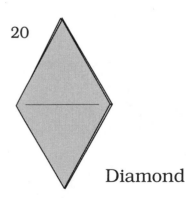

Diamond

Heart

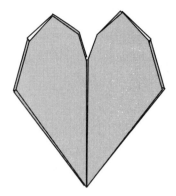

The term "heart" is also used to describe this suit in both French ("coeur") and in German ("Herz") as well as English. In Italian, it is called a cup ("coppa").

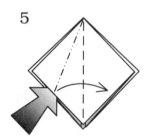

1

Fold and unfold along the diagonals.

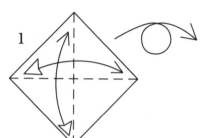

2

Fold and unfold.

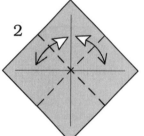

3

Collapse the square by bringing the four corners together.

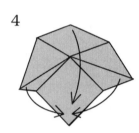

4

This is a three-dimensional intermediate step.

5

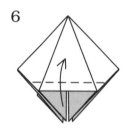

Squash-fold, repeat behind.

6

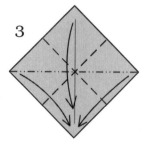

There are no guide lines for this fold, repeat behind.

7

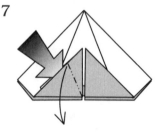

Squash-fold.

8

Note the bold lines are parallel. Repeat on the right and behind.

9

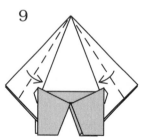

10

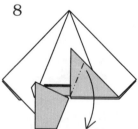

Unfold everything.

11

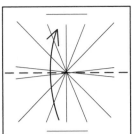

12

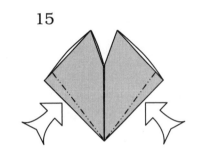

Repeat behind. The folds through step 9 will be refolded.

13

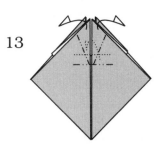

Refold steps 6–8, repeat behind.

14

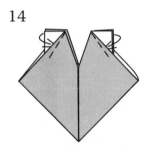

Before continuing, check that this is the same as step 9 but from the inside. Fold both layers together on the left and right sides.

15

Reverse folds.

16

Reverse folds.

17

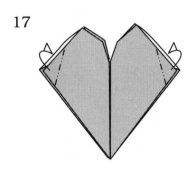

Repeat behind.

18

Heart

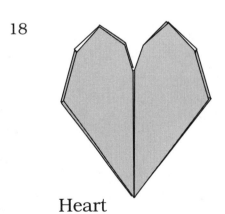

Spade

The spade symbol is known as a pike ("pique") in French, a leaf ("Grün") in German, and a sword ("spada") in Italian.

1

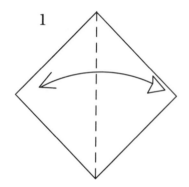

Fold and unfold.

2

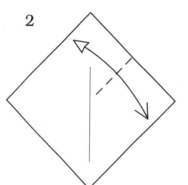

Fold and unfold.

3

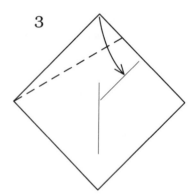

Fold the corner to the center line.

4

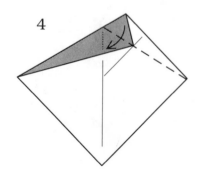

5

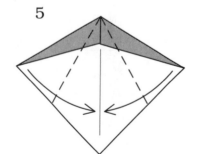

6

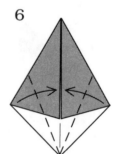

7

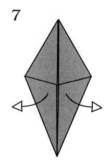

Unfold.

8

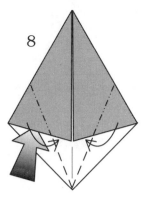

Reverse folds.

9

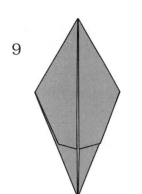

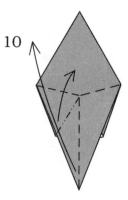

10

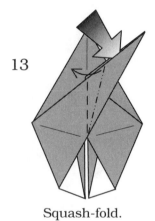

Rabbit-ear.

11

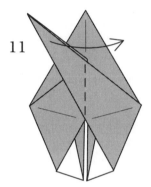

12

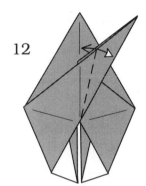

Fold and unfold.

13

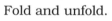

Squash-fold.

14

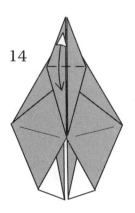

Fold and unfold.

15

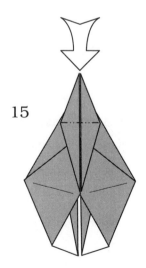

Sink.

16

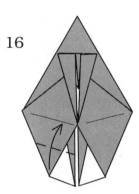

Fold to the crease.

17

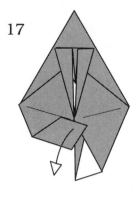

Unfold.

18

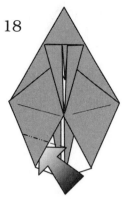

Squash-fold.

19

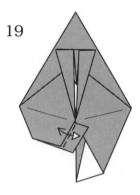

Fold and unfold.

20

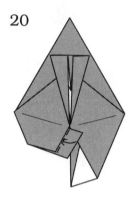

Tuck.

21

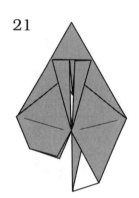

Repeat steps 16–20
on the right.

22

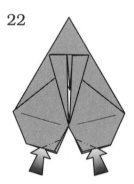

Reverse folds.

23

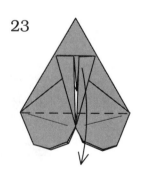

24

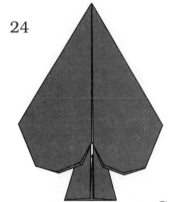

Spade

Club

The club symbol is known as a clover ("trèfle") in French, an acorn ("Eichel") in German, and a rod ("bastone") in Italian.

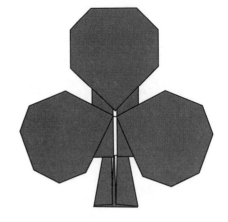

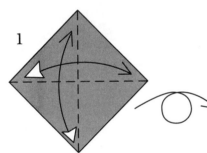

1 Fold and unfold along the diagonals.

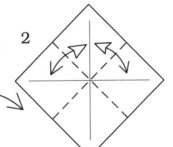

2 Fold and unfold.

3 Collapse the square by bringing the four corners together.

4 This is a three-dimensional intermediate step.

5 Fold and unfold, repeat behind.

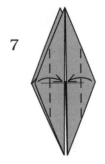

6 Petal-fold, repeat behind.

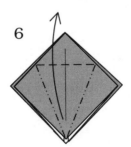

7 Repeat behind.

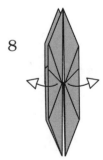

8 Unfold, repeat behind.

9

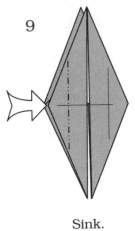

Sink.

10

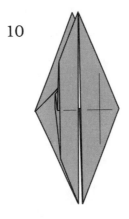

Sink the three other sides,

11

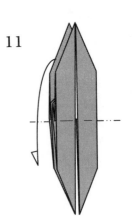

12

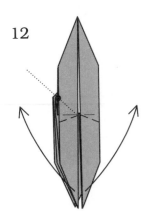

Valley-fold up to 45°.

13

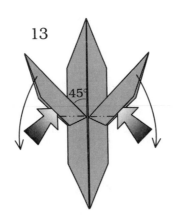

Squash folds.

14

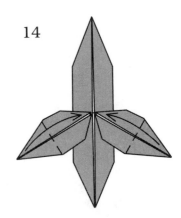

15

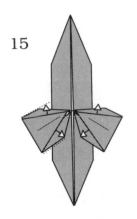

Pull out.

16

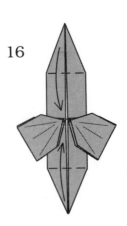

17

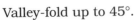

Pull out at the top,
unfold at the bottom.

18

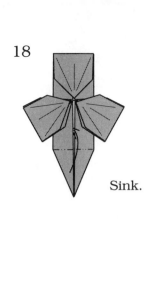

Sink.

19

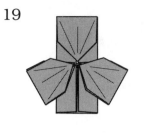

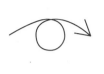
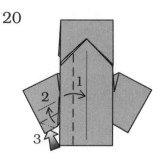

20

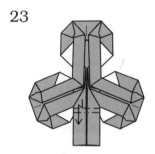

Fold in order, 3 is
a squash fold.

21

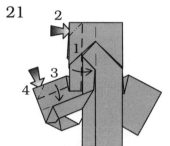

Fold in order, 2 and 4
are squash folds.

22

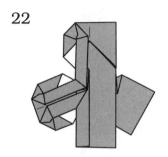

Repeat steps 20–21
on the right.

23

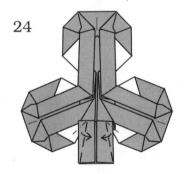

24

Squash folds.

25

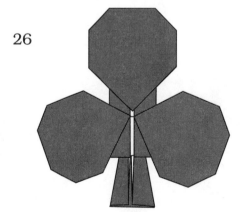

26

Club

The Chinese Zodiac

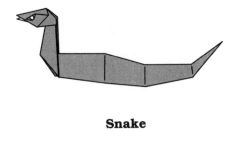

Snake

Chinese Dragon

Rabbit

The Chinese and Japanese zodiac, much like that of the West, is steeped in a long tradition of mythology and predicting human personality traits, its roots having been traced back to ancient Chinese and Indian origin. The system consists of twelve cylces, each marked by a particular animal.

As one traditional story goes, on New Year's Day, many years ago, Buddha called all the animals of the world to him. Having promised any who came a gift for their devotion, Buddha gave each of the twelve animals who arrived to pay tribute a year which would be named after them. The twelve animals, and hence the twelve years of the zodiac cycle were: the rat, ox, tiger, rabbit, dragon, snake, horse, sheep, monkey, rooster, dog, and boar. Having come to Buddha in this fashion, this is the order that the zodiac cycle follows. In 1900, a new cycle was begun with the year of the rat. Although it ended in 1912 with the year of the boar, one can easily determine their own birth year by counting from 1900.

Tiger

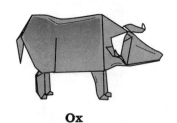

Ox

Rat

Horse

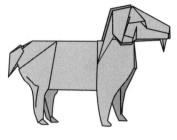

Ram

Monkey

Rooster

Upon receipt of a year of their own, each animal imprinted it with its own distinct characteristics. According to belief, people born within each of these years will naturally possess aspects of these characteristics. From knowledge of which sign you were born under, the zodiac can supposedly tell about your personal, romantic, financial, social, and even political traits. The year of birth can even determine weaknesses, temptations, and auspicious marriages for people. Eastern fortunetellers claim that by knowing a person's birth year, they can give advice to adapt and even improve their lives.

Dog

Boar

Rat

1900, 1912, 1924, 1936, 1948, 1960, 1972, 1984, 1996 12008

People born in the year of the rat are charming, determined, fussy, and frugal. They have a tendency to spend too much money on people whom they love but who do not return their affection. Rat people are quick to anger, but are able to control their temper. They are honest and ambitious and do not give up as easily as the monkey. Rats also like to gossip and are therefore good at making temporary friendships. As rats age, they will make mistakes involving love, but will ultimately end up living well. For long term relationships, those born in the years of the monkey, dragon, and ox are good for the rat while the horse will lead to disaster, even early death.

Rat

Chinese	Japanese
"Shǔ"	"Nezumi"

Year of the Rat

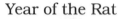

Chinese	Japanese
"Zǐ"	"Ne"

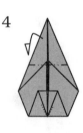

1

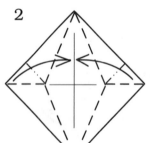

Fold and unfold.

2

Rabbit ears.

3

Divide in thirds.

4

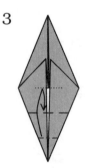

Fold to the bottom.

5

Fold and unfold.

6

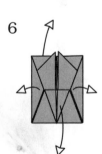

Unfold.

7

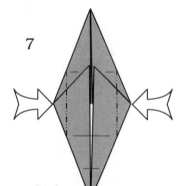

Sink.

8

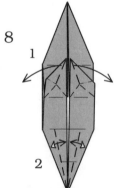

1. Rabbit-ear the legs.
2. Fold and unfold the tail.

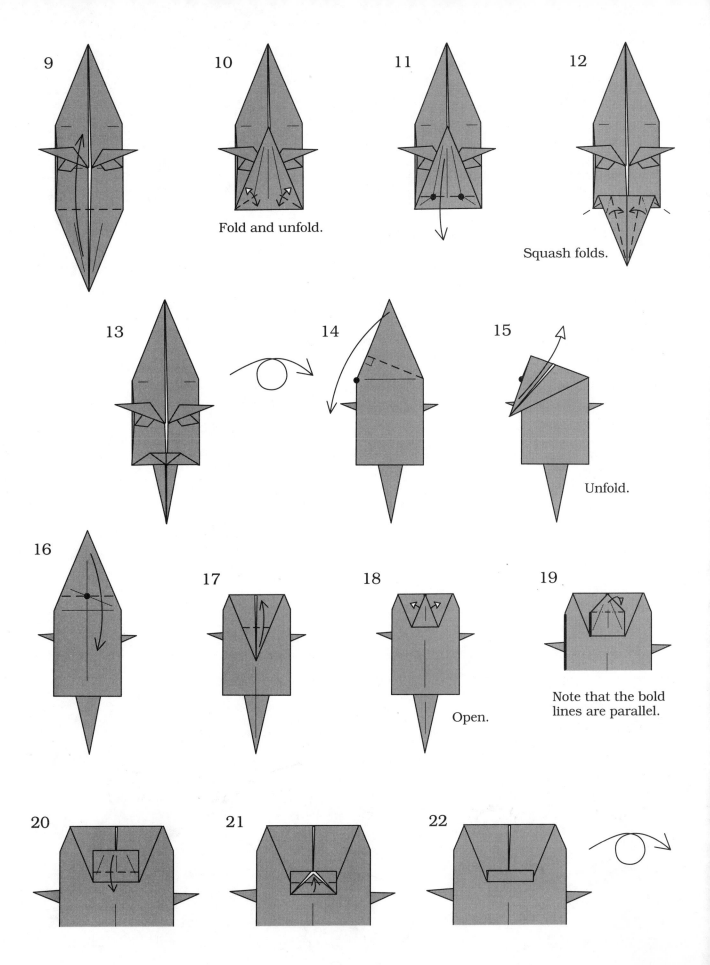

9

10

Fold and unfold.

11

12

Squash folds.

13

14

15

Unfold.

16

17

18

Open.

19

Note that the bold
lines are parallel.

20

21

22

Rat 23

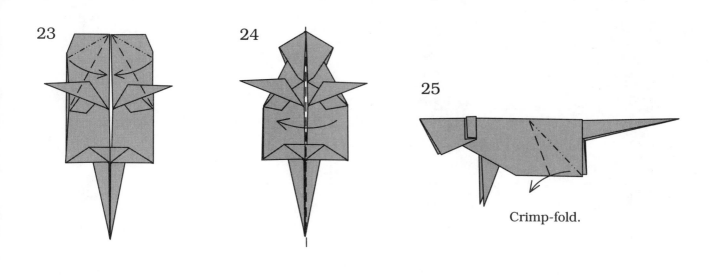

23

24

25

Crimp-fold.

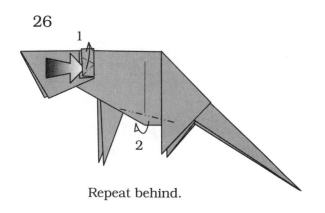

26

1

2

Repeat behind.

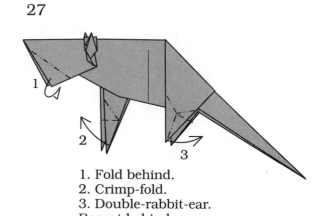

27

1

2

3

1. Fold behind.
2. Crimp-fold.
3. Double-rabbit-ear.
Repeat behind.

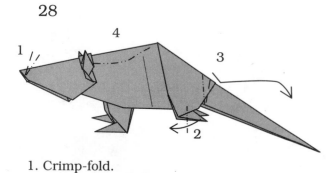

28

1

4

3

2

1. Crimp-fold.
2. Reverse-fold, repeat behind.
3. Crimp-fold and curl the tail.
4. Shape the back.

29

Rat

Ox

牛

Chinese   Japanese
"Niú"   "Ushi"

Year of the Ox

丑

Chinese   Japanese
   ˇ   "Ushi"
"Cho u"

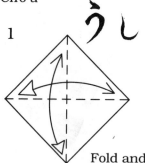

Ox

1901, 1913, 1925, 1937, 1949, 1961, 1973, 1985, 1997, 2009

Those born in the year of the ox tend to be silent, patient, and confident. Although they rarely speak, when required to do so they are often eloquent. Ox people are also very dexterous and can do virtually anything with their hands. Oxen can be stubborn and short tempered, and it is unwise to confront an angry one. Their stubbornness is sometimes good though, because it causes them to try their hardest, and not to fail in anything. Oxen do not take relationships with the opposite sex too seriously, and this often leads to problems for them. Despite their difficulties with marriage, an ox would marry well with a snake or rooster but not with a ram.

1

Fold and unfold
along the diagonals.

2

3

Fold and unfold.

4

Fold and unfold.

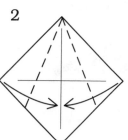

5

Squash-fold.

6

Squash-fold.

7

Squash-fold.

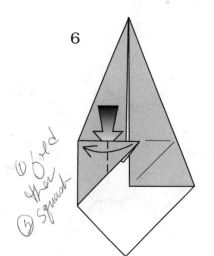

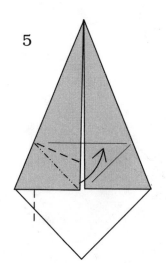

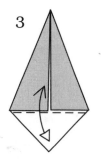

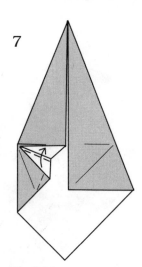

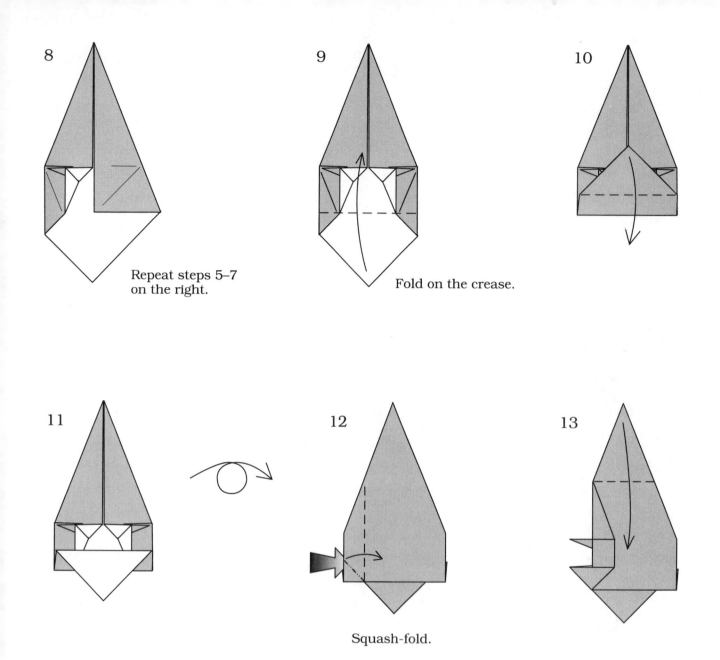

8

Repeat steps 5–7
on the right.

9

Fold on the crease.

10

11

12

Squash-fold.

13

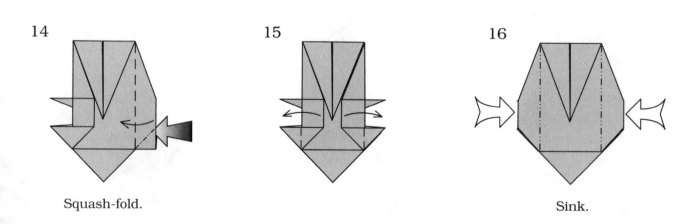

14

Squash-fold.

15

16

Sink.

17

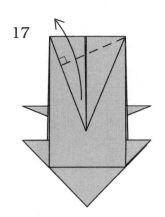

18

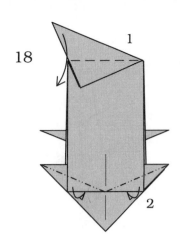

19

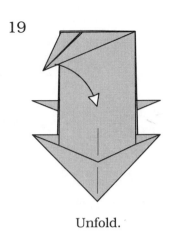

Unfold.

20

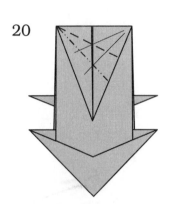

Fold and unfold.

21

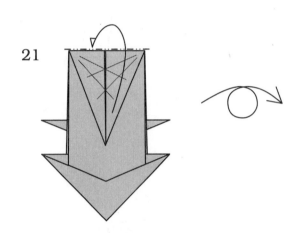

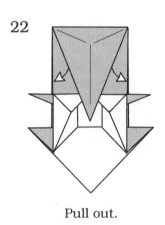

22

Pull out.

23

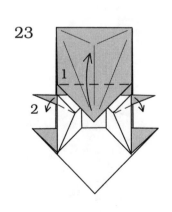

24

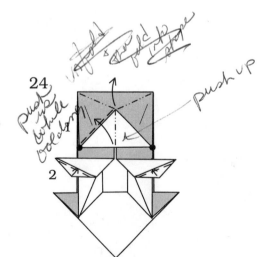

1. Bring the dots together
   at the head.
2. Tuck inside for the legs.

25

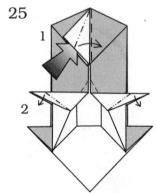

Squash-fold at the head.

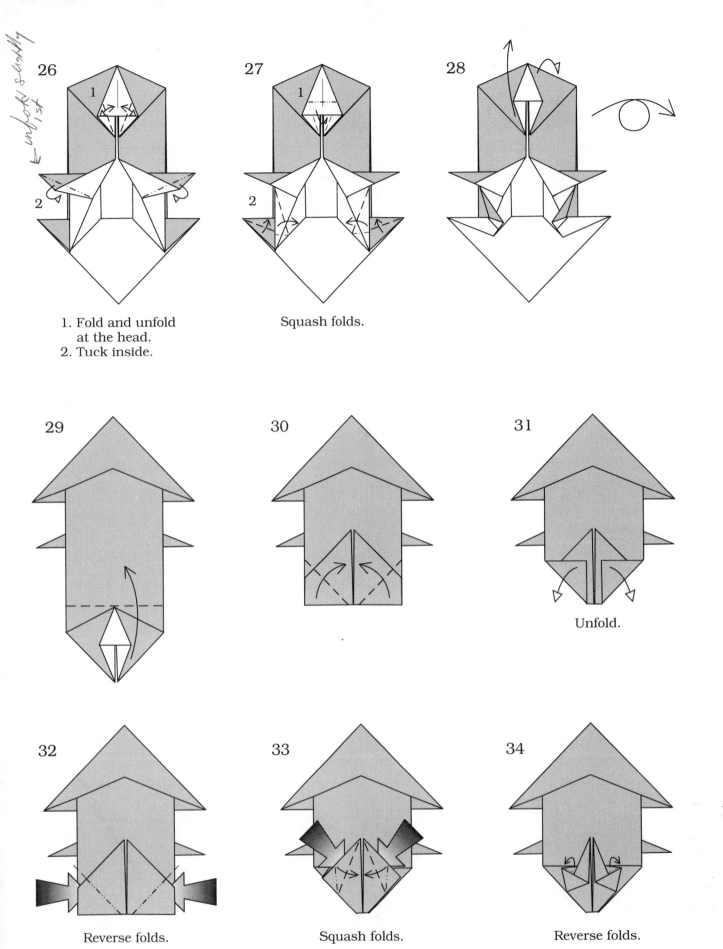

26

1. Fold and unfold at the head.
2. Tuck inside.

27

Squash folds.

28

29

30

31

Unfold.

32

Reverse folds.

33

Squash folds.

34

Reverse folds.

35

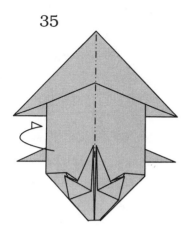

36

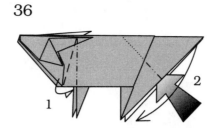

1. Crimp-fold the head.
2. Reverse-fold the tail.

37

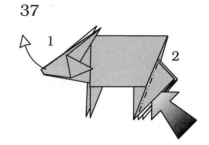

1. Unfold the head.
2. Reverse-fold the tail, repeat behind.

38

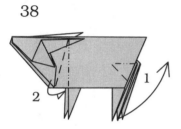

1. Crimp-fold.
2. Tuck inside the pocket for this crimp fold.

39

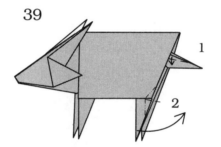

Repeat behind.

40

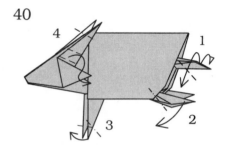

1. Outside-reverse-fold.
2. Reverse-fold.
3. Crimp-fold.
4. Shape the horns.
Repeat behind.

41

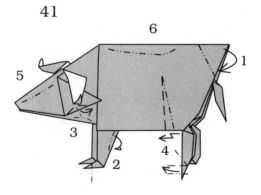

Repeat behind.

42

Ox

Tiger

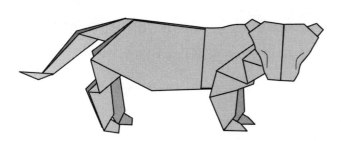

Tiger

Chinese   Japanese
"Hǔ"   "Tora"

1902, 1914, 1926, 1938, 1950, 1962, 1974, 1986, 1998 ₁₂/₁₀

Those born in the year of the tiger tend to be tempramental, sensitive, pensive, and sympathetic towards friends. Often they have problems with authority, and can be stubborn, selfish, and mean. People who are not friends can sometimes be subject to suspicion by tiger people. Tigers are not as good at making decisions as monkey people, but get more credit than they deserve. In the plus column though, tigers are very brave. As with monkeys, they will run into problems later in life. Those born in the years of the dog and the horse make good relationships with tigers, and tigers should avoid monkeys.

Year of the Tiger

Chinese   Japanese
"Yín"   "Tora"

1
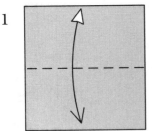

2
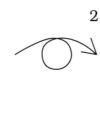

3
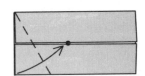

4
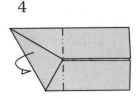

5
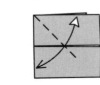

Fold and unfold.

6
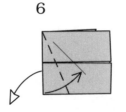

Fold to the crease while unfolding the paper from behind.

7
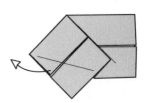

Unfold.

8
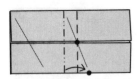

9
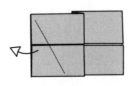

Unfold.

10
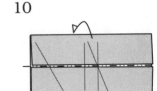

11

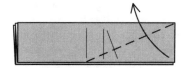

Repeat behind.

12

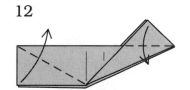

Repeat behind.

13

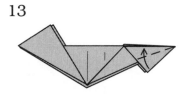

Repeat behind.

14

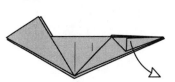

Unfold, repeat behind.

15

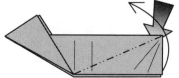

Reverse-fold, repeat behind.

16

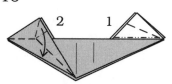

1. Continue reverse folding.
2. Rabbit-ear on the left.
Repeat behind.

17

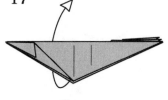

Open.

18

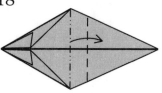

19

Reverse folds.

20

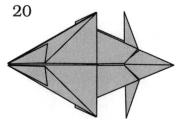

21

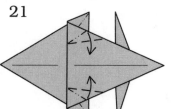

Squash folds.

22

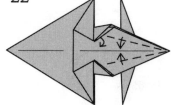

Slide out.

Tiger 31

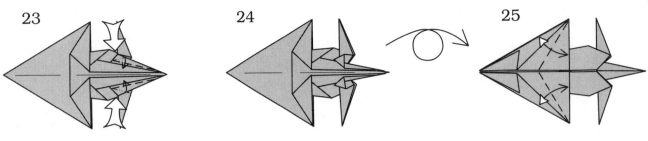

23

24

25

Spread squash folds.

Fold and unfold.

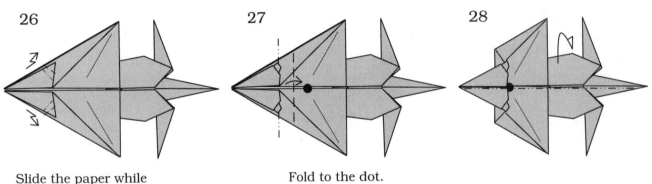

26

27

28

Slide the paper while
doing the reverse folds.

Fold to the dot.

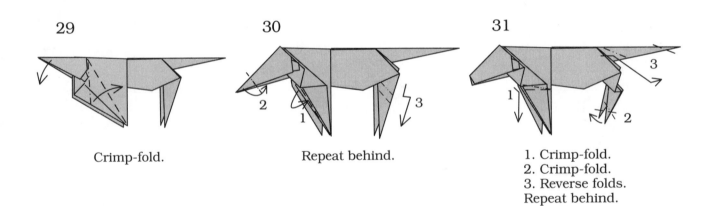

29

30

31

Crimp-fold.

Repeat behind.

1. Crimp-fold.
2. Crimp-fold.
3. Reverse folds.
Repeat behind.

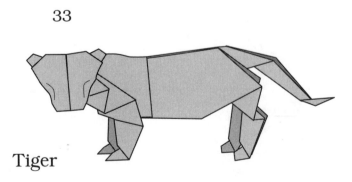

32

33

Repeat behind.

Tiger

Rabbit

Rabbit

Chinese
"Tù"

Japanese
"Usagi"

うさぎ

Year of the Rabbit

Chinese
"Mǎo"

Japanese
"U"

1903, 1915, 1927, 1939, 1951, 1963, 1975, 1987, 1999, 2111

Rabbits are lucky, especially in terms of money. They make good business people and are very eloquent. The downside of their eloquence is that they like to gossip, but at least they are always tactful. Rabbits have many talents, and are well liked and admired. They also are very slow to anger, and they love their family although they seem oddly detached. In general, rabbits are peaceful and conservative, yet not very knowledgeable. Throughout their lives rabbits will stay relatively peaceful if they do not take on anything too big. Rabbits form good marriages with rams and boars but not with roosters.

1

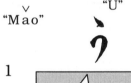

2

3

Fold the corners to the center line.

4

5

6

7

Fold and unfold.

8

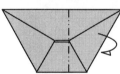

Fold to the crease while unfolding the paper from behind.

9

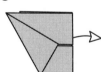

Unfold.

10

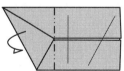

11

Unfold.

12

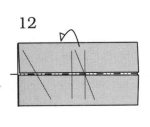

13

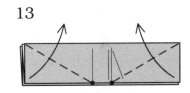

Repeat behind.

14

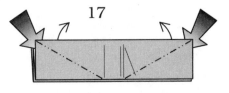

Repeat behind.

15

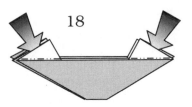

Repeat behind.

16

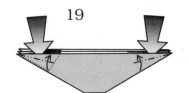

Unfold, repeat behind.

17

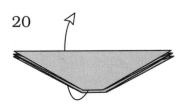

Reverse folds, repeat behind.

18

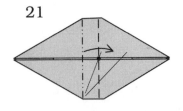

Reverse folds, repeat behind.

19

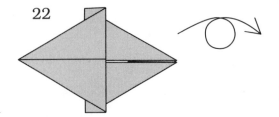

Reverse folds, repeat behind.

20

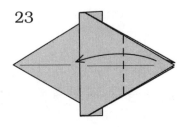

Open.

21

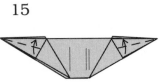

22

23

24

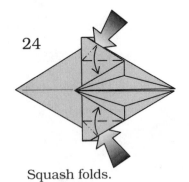

Squash folds.

25

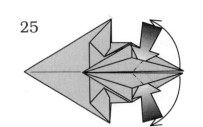

Reverse folds.

26

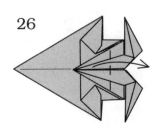

27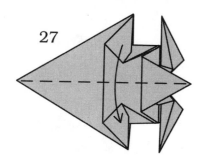

28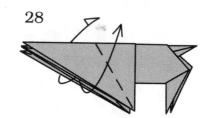

Outside-reverse-fold.

29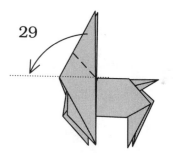

Outside-reverse-fold.

30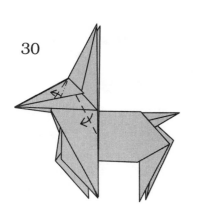

Repeat behind.

31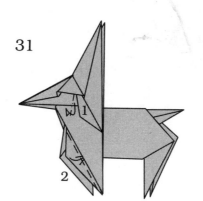

Repeat behind.

32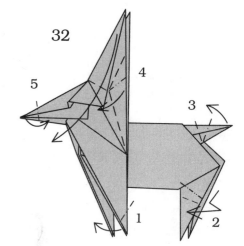

Repeat behind.

33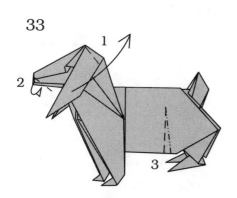

Repeat behind.

34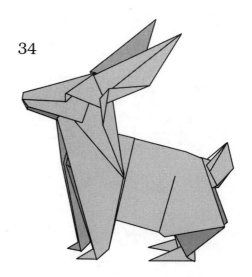

Rabbit

Rabbit 35

Chinese Dragon

Dragon

Chinese "Lóng" Japanese "Ryū"

りゅう

1904, 1916, 1928, 1940, 1952, 1964, 1976, 1988, 2000, 2112

People born in the dragon years have enthusiasm, sincerity, sensitivity, and courage. They also have a hot temper, stubbornness, and a big mouth; this is not to say that dragons gossip. Dragons are very sympathetic, and they are slightly gullible because of this. They have a tendency to worry a lot, sometimes about other people, but mostly about nothing. In general, people like dragons, but dragons are still often lonely, marrying late in life, if at all. A dragon should look for someone born in the year of the monkey or rat for a relationship, but should keep away from dogs.

Year of the Dragon

Chinese "Chén" Japanese "Tatsu"

たつ

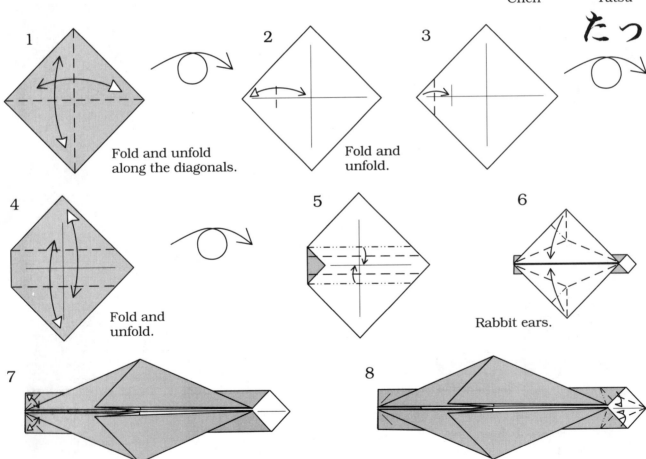

1 Fold and unfold along the diagonals.

2 Fold and unfold.

3

4 Fold and unfold.

5

6 Rabbit ears.

7 Fold and unfold.

8

9

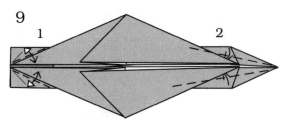

1   2

Fold and unfold on the left.

10

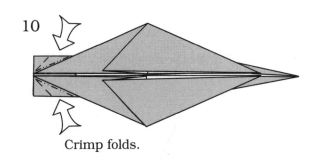

Crimp folds.

11

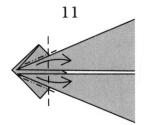

Squash folds.

12

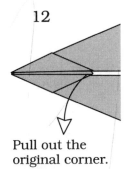

Pull out the original corner.

13

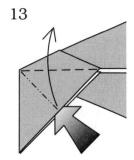

Squash-fold.

14

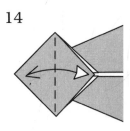

Fold and unfold.

15

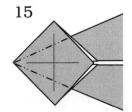

Reverse folds.

16

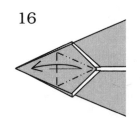

Petal-fold.

17

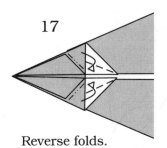

Reverse folds.

18

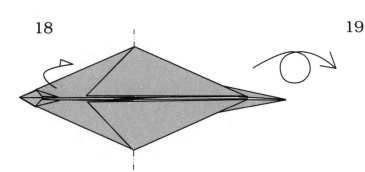

19

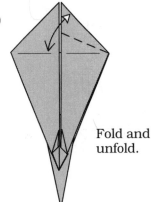

Fold and unfold.

20

Chinese Dragon 37

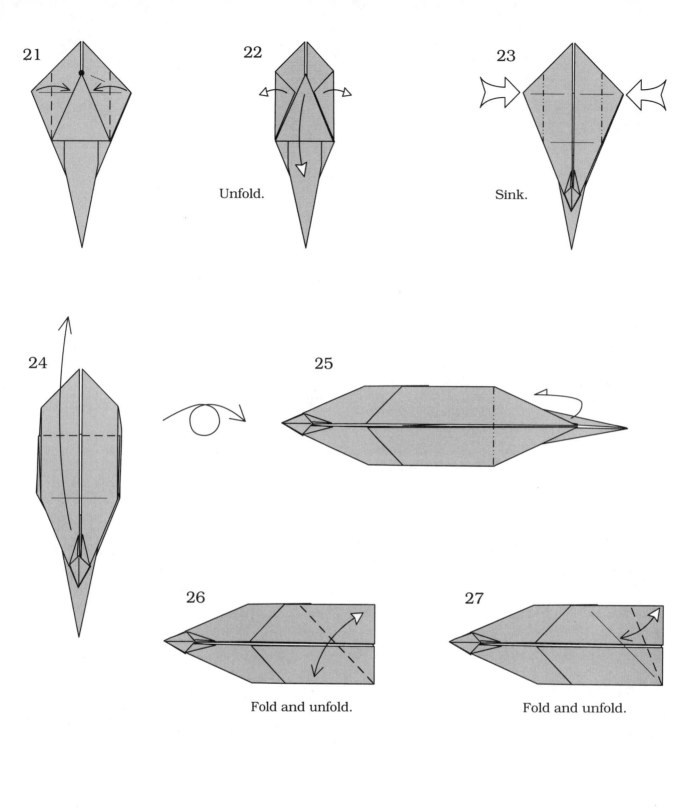

21

22

Unfold.

23

Sink.

24

25

26

Fold and unfold.

27

Fold and unfold.

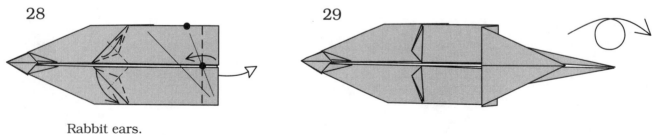

28

Rabbit ears.

29

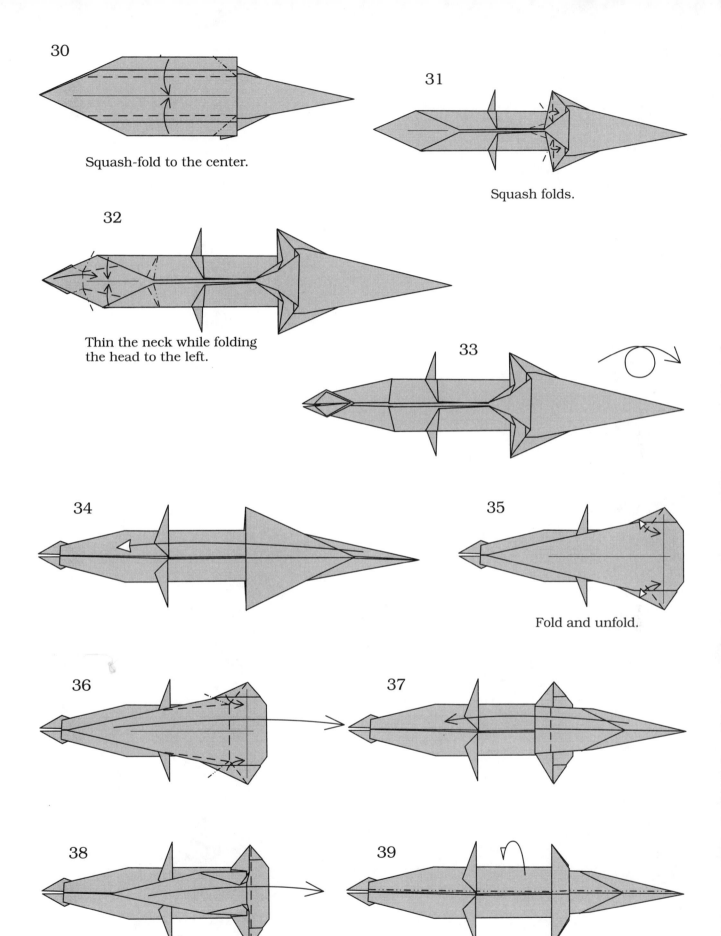

30

Squash-fold to the center.

31

Squash folds.

32

Thin the neck while folding the head to the left.

33

34

35

Fold and unfold.

36

37

38

39

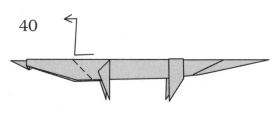

40

Outside-reverse-fold.

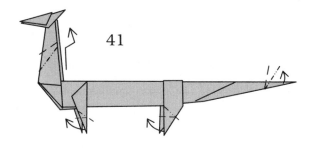

41

Crimp-fold the neck, feet, and open the tail.

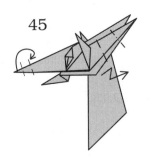

42

Repeat behind.

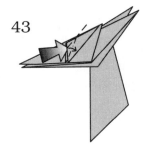

43

Spread-squash-fold
the eye, repeat behind.

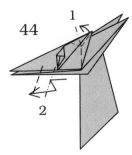

44

1

2

1. Rabbit-ear,
   repeat behind.
2. Crimp-fold.

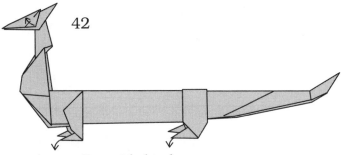

45

Repeat behind.

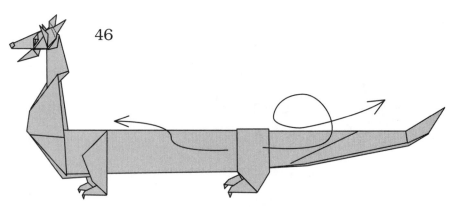

46

Curl the body and tail.

47

Chinese Dragon

Snake

Chinese "Shé" Japanese "Hebi"

Year of the Snake

Chinese "Si" Japanese "Mi"

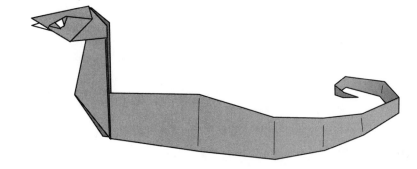

1905, 1917, 1929, 1941, 1953, 1965, 1977, 1989, 2001

Snake people are not very verbal, but are people of action. They are wise and sympathetic, and do try to help people, as long as it does not involve loaning. Snake people will always be lucky with regard to money, but do not like to share it. Snakes are usually perfectionists; they hate to fail in anything they do. Although snakes tend to be gifted with physical beauty, they often have problems with marriage, especially extra-marital affairs. Snakes marry well with oxen and roosters. They should be wary of the boar.

1

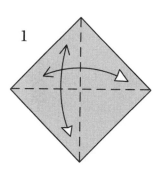

Fold and unfold along the diagonals.

2

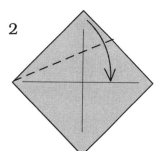

3

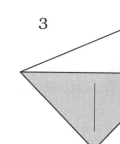

4

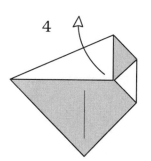

Unfold.

5

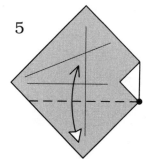

Fold up and unfold.

6

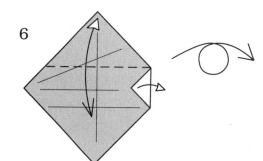

Fold and unfold.

7

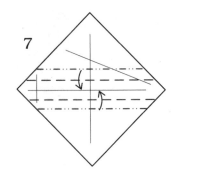

8

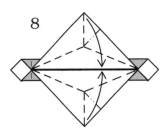

Rabbit ears.

9

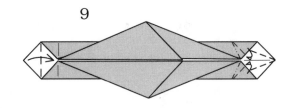

10

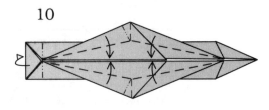

Rabbit ears.

11

Fold in thirds.

12

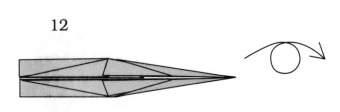

13

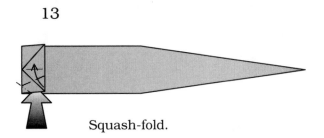

Squash-fold.

14

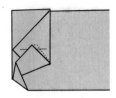

Pull out.

15

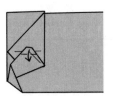

16

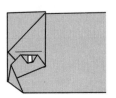

Repeat steps 13–15 above.

42   *Mythological Creatures and the Chinese Zodiac*

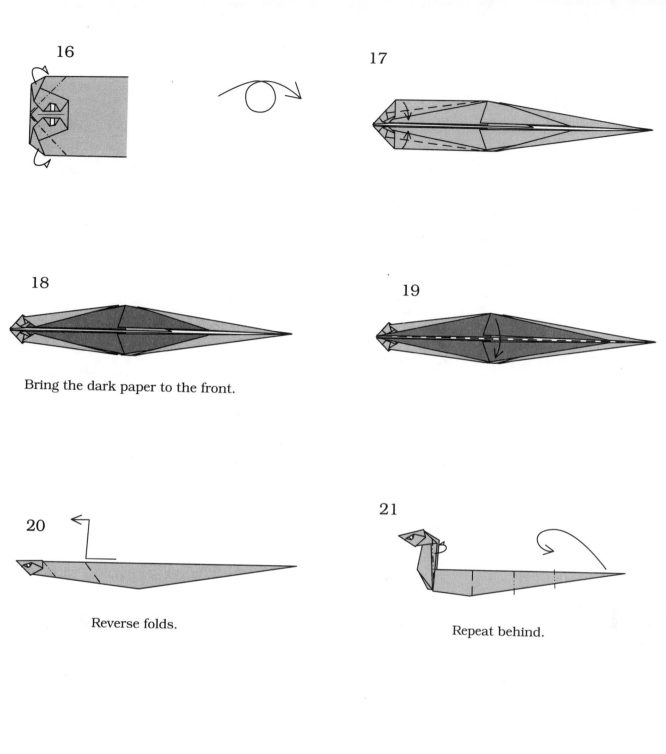

16

17

18

Bring the dark paper to the front.

19

20

Reverse folds.

21

Repeat behind.

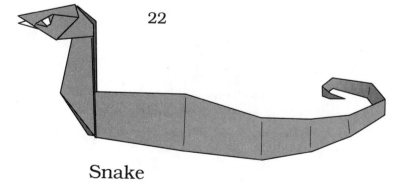

22

Snake

Horse

1906, 1918, 1930, 1942, 1954, 1966, 1978, 1990, 2002

A person born in the year of the horse is normally "a people person." Horses are popular, happy, and talkative, possibly too much so. They are also very independent and hot-blooded, and tend to disregard advice. Horses anger quickly, and with regards to their passions can be virtually unaware of anything else. They often fail when involved in long-term projects. They are quick-witted and wise, good with money, and skillful with their hands. Much of their appeal, however, is based on appearances, and they are often weak and unconfident when it comes to members of the opposite sex. Horses mix well with tigers and dogs, but ought to stay away from rats.

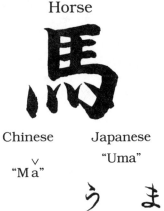

Year of the Horse

午

Chinese · Japanese
"Wu" "Uma"

う ま

1

Fold and unfold.

2

3

Fold and unfold.

4

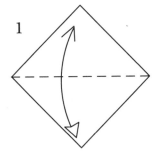

Fold and unfold.

5

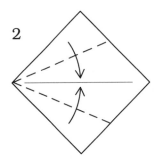

Fold the left tip half way between the creases.

6

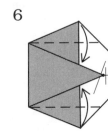

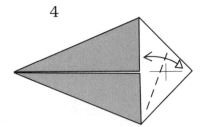

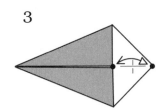

7 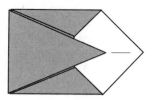 8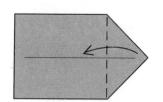

9 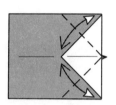 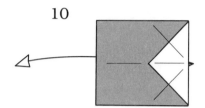 10 11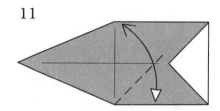

Fold and unfold.   Unfold.   Fold up and unfold.

12 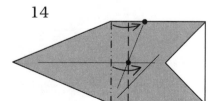 13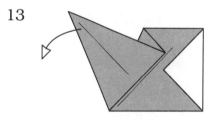

Unfold.

14 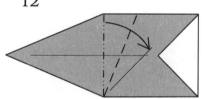 15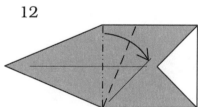

16

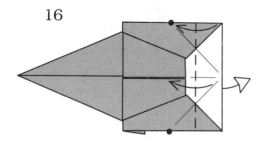

17

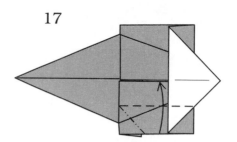

Squash-fold to the center.

18

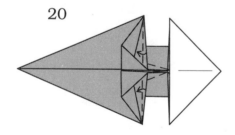

Pull out the corner.

19

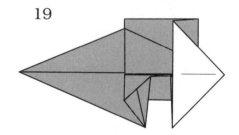

Repeat steps 17–18 above.

20

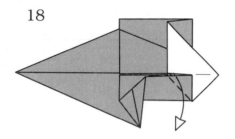

Squash folds.

21

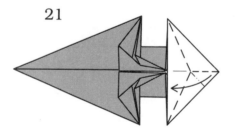

Rabbit-ear.

22

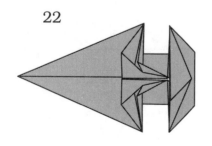

23

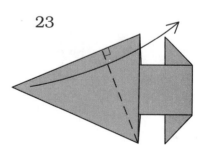

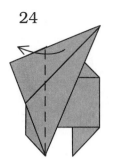

24

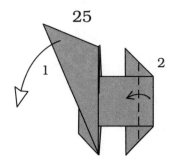

25

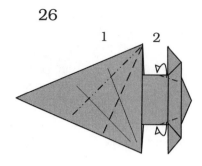

26

1. Fold and unfold.
2. Fold behind.

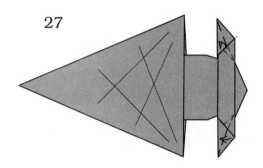

27

Reverse folds.

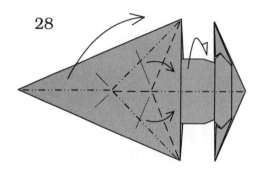

28

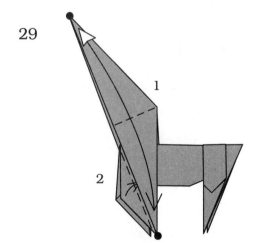

29

1. Fold and unfold.
2. Tuck, repeat behind.

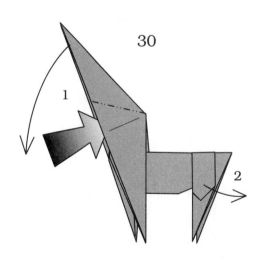

30

1. Reverse-fold.
2. Slide out the tail.

Horse 47

31

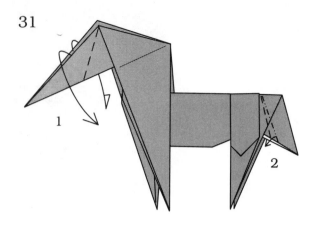

1. Outside-reverse-fold.
2. Crimp-fold.

32

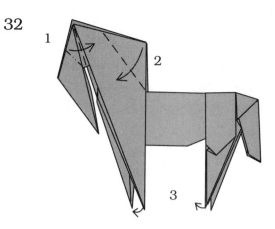

1. Crimp-fold.
2. Valley-fold.
3. Form the hooves.
Repeat behind.

33

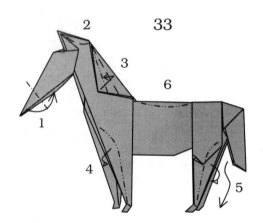

Repeat behind.

34

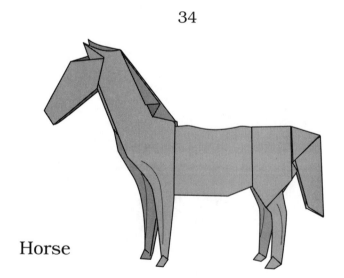

Horse

Ram

Ram

羊

Chinese "Yáng" Japanese "Hitsuji"

ひつじ

Year of the Ram

未

Chinese "Wèi" Japanese "Hitsuji"

ひつじ

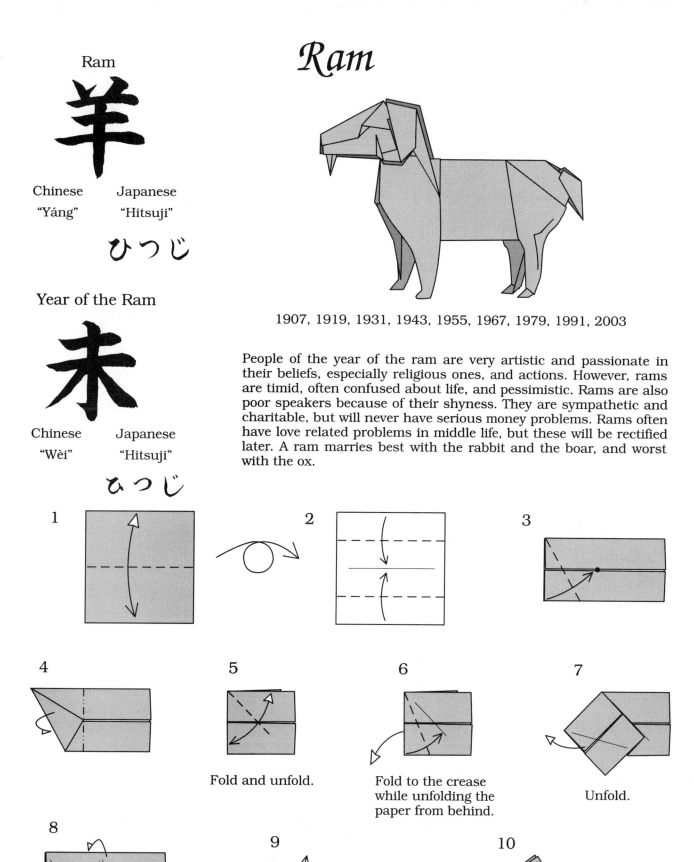

1907, 1919, 1931, 1943, 1955, 1967, 1979, 1991, 2003

People of the year of the ram are very artistic and passionate in their beliefs, especially religious ones, and actions. However, rams are timid, often confused about life, and pessimistic. Rams are also poor speakers because of their shyness. They are sympathetic and charitable, but will never have serious money problems. Rams often have love related problems in middle life, but these will be rectified later. A ram marries best with the rabbit and the boar, and worst with the ox.

1

2

3

4

5

Fold and unfold.

6

Fold to the crease while unfolding the paper from behind.

7

Unfold.

8

9

Repeat behind.

10

Repeat behind.

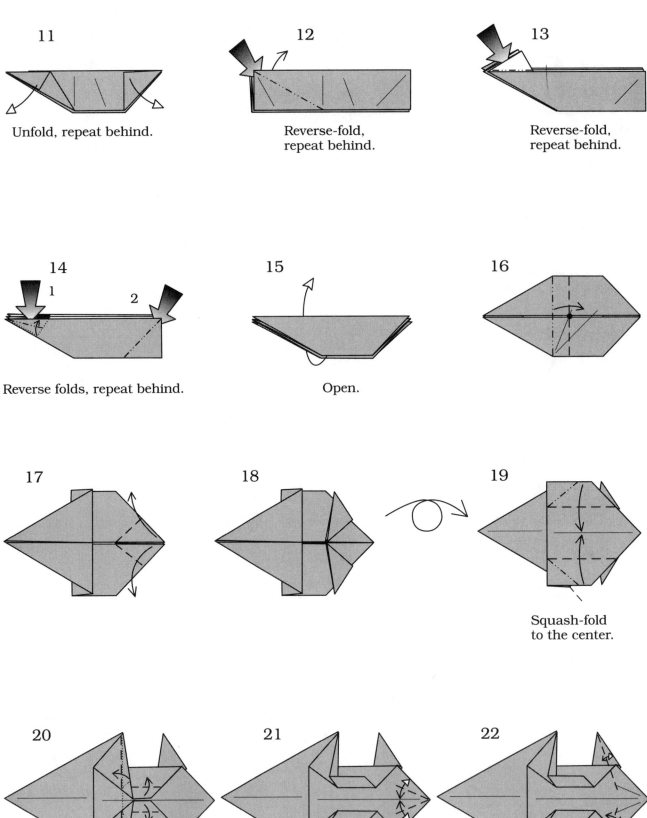

11 Unfold, repeat behind.

12 Reverse-fold, repeat behind.

13 Reverse-fold, repeat behind.

14 Reverse folds, repeat behind.

15 Open.

16

17

18

19 Squash-fold to the center.

20 Squash folds.

21 Fold and unfold.

22 Fold at an angle of one third and unfold.

23

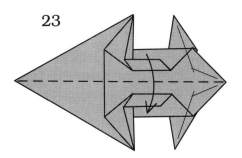

24

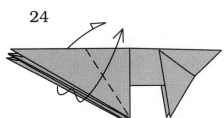

Outside-reverse-fold.

25

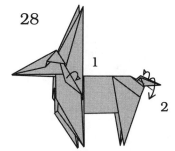

1. Outside-reverse-fold.
2. Fold along the creases.

26

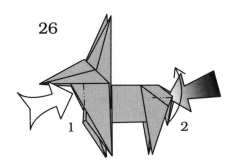

1. Sink.
2. Reverse-fold.

27

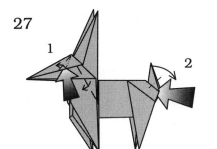

1. Form the eye.
2. Reverse-fold.
Repeat behind.

28

1. Fold behind.
2. Outside-reverse-fold.
Repeat behind.

29

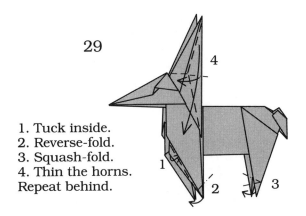

1. Tuck inside.
2. Reverse-fold.
3. Squash-fold.
4. Thin the horns.
Repeat behind.

31

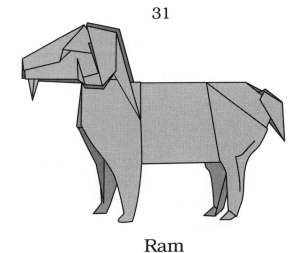

Ram

30

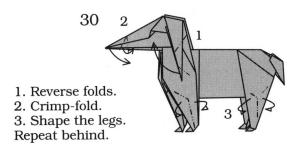

1. Reverse folds.
2. Crimp-fold.
3. Shape the legs.
Repeat behind.

Monkey

Monkey

Chinese "Yuán"   Japanese "Saru"

1908, 1920, 1932, 1944, 1956, 1968, 1980, 1992, 2004

People born in the year of the monkey generally are highly intelligent, creative, have excellent memories, and are good at solving problems. Unfortunately, they lack the sense of drive of the people born in the year of the rat, and are easily discouraged, often giving up before they start something. They tend to consider others inferior, and are sometimes condescending. On the good side, those born in the year of the monkey are excellent decision makers and use common sense. Later in life, monkeys will lose some of their skills, and will have problems with members of the opposite sex. As a monkey, look to the dragon and the rat for good friendships or marriage, but stay away from the tiger.

Year of the Monkey

Chinese "Shēn"   Japanese "Saru"

1

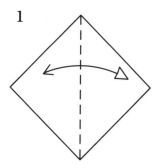

Fold and unfold.

2

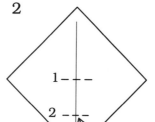

Fold and unfold in half for creases 1 and 2.

3

4

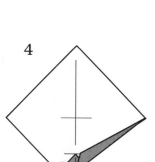

Pull out.

5

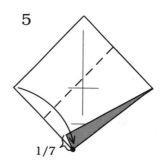

1/7

This folding method divides the paper into sevenths.

6

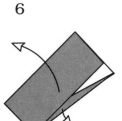

Unfold.

7

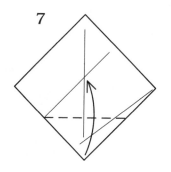

8

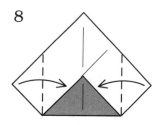

9

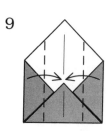

10

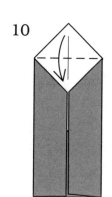

11

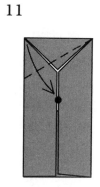

Fold the corner to
the center line.

12

13

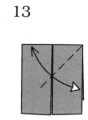

Fold and unfold.

14

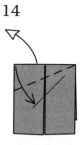

Fold to the crease
while unfolding the
paper from behind.

15

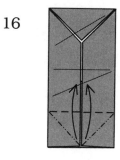

Unfold.

16

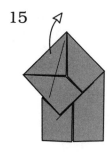

Squash folds.

17

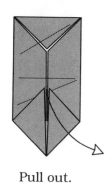

Pull out.

18

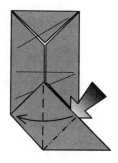

Squash-fold.

19

Fold and unfold.

20

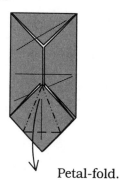

Petal-fold.

21

Monkey 53

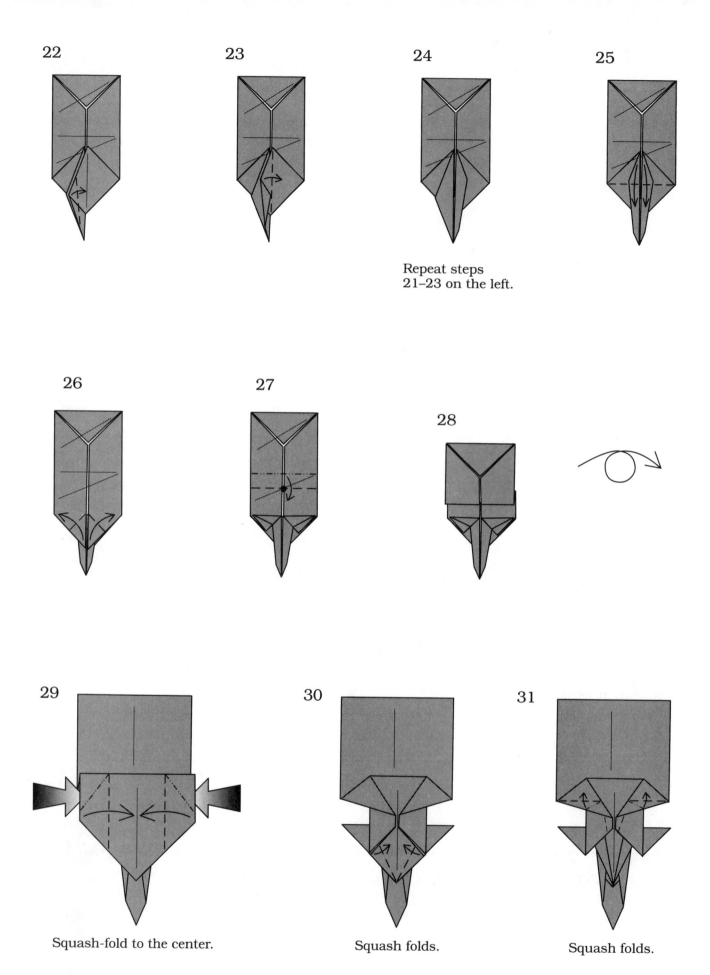

22

23

24

Repeat steps
21–23 on the left.

25

26

27

28

29

Squash-fold to the center.

30

Squash folds.

31

Squash folds.

54 *Mythological Creatures and the Chinese Zodiac*

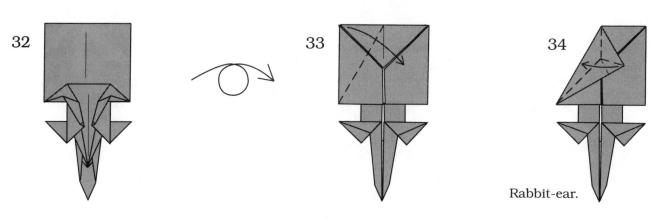

32

33

34

Rabbit-ear.

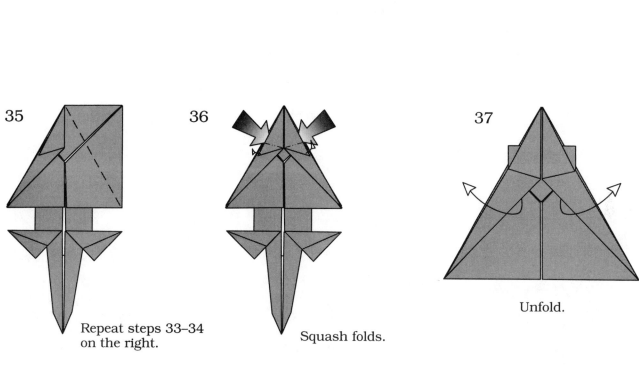

35

Repeat steps 33–34
on the right.

36

Squash folds.

37

Unfold.

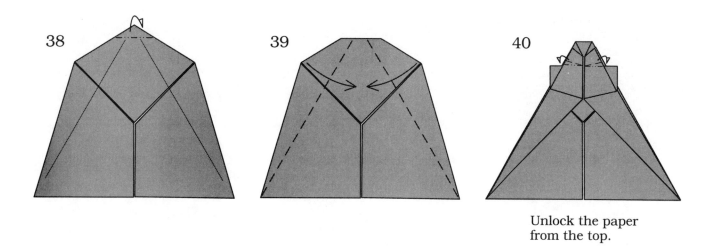

38

39

40

Unlock the paper
from the top.

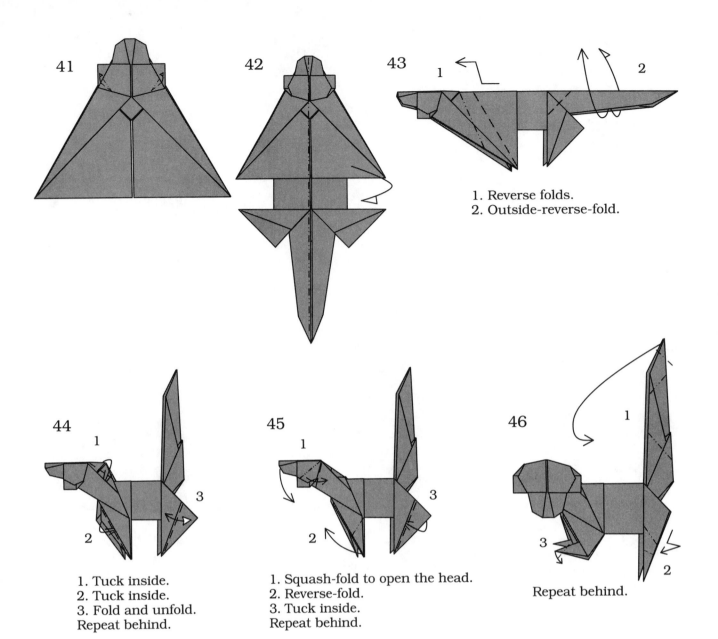

41

42

43

1. Reverse folds.
2. Outside-reverse-fold.

44

1. Tuck inside.
2. Tuck inside.
3. Fold and unfold.
Repeat behind.

45

1. Squash-fold to open the head.
2. Reverse-fold.
3. Tuck inside.
Repeat behind.

46

Repeat behind.

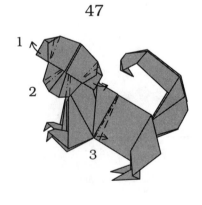

47

48

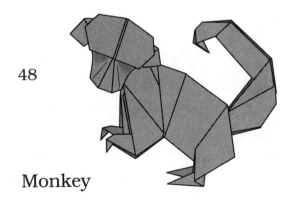

Monkey

Rooster

Rooster

Chinese   Japanese

"Jī"   "Niwatori"

にわとり

Year of the Rooster

Chinese   Japanese

"Yŏu"   "Tori"

とり

1909, 1921, 1933, 1945, 1957, 1969, 1981, 1993, 2005

Rooster people are pensive and devoted, but sometimes they "bite off more than they can chew," and get disappointed when they cannot finish. Roosters are loners, because they do not trust others. In conflicts they think they are right, and everyone who does not agree is wrong. They are selfish, tactless, and somewhat immature, and have alternating good fortune and bad luck throughout their lives. They are not very good with people. Snakes and oxen are the best marriage partners for the rooster, but never the rabbit.

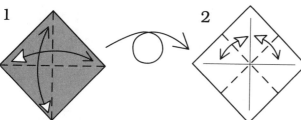

1

Fold and unfold along the diagonals.

2

Fold and unfold.

3

Collapse the square by bringing the four corners together.

4

This is a three-dimensional intermediate step.

5

Kite-fold, repeat behind.

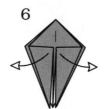

6

Unfold, repeat behind.

7

Fold and unfold, repeat behind.

8

Repeat behind.

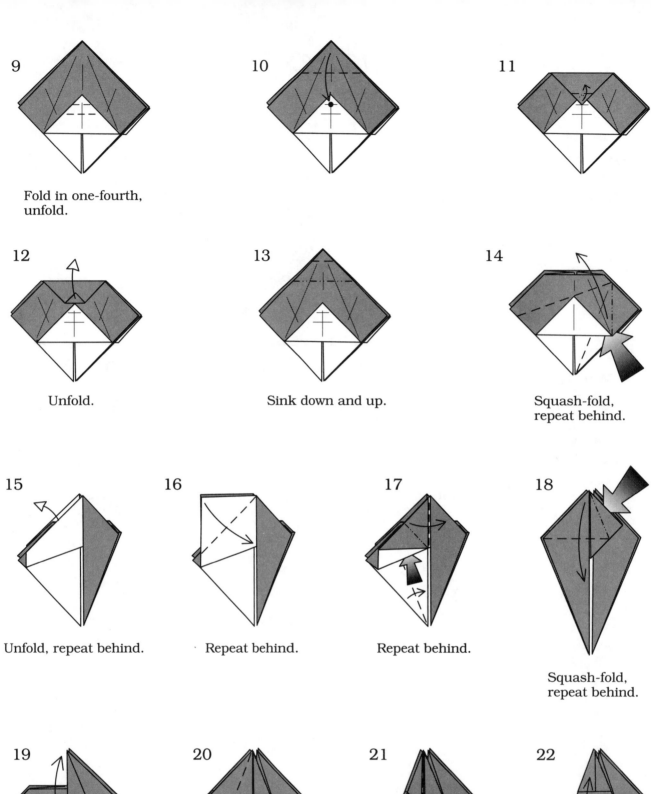

9

Fold in one-fourth, unfold.

10

11

12

Unfold.

13

Sink down and up.

14

Squash-fold, repeat behind.

15

Unfold, repeat behind.

16

Repeat behind.

17

Repeat behind.

18

Squash-fold, repeat behind.

19

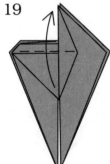

Repeat behind.

20

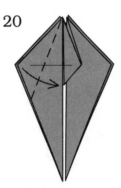

Repeat behind.

21

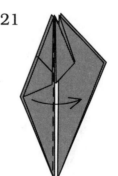

22

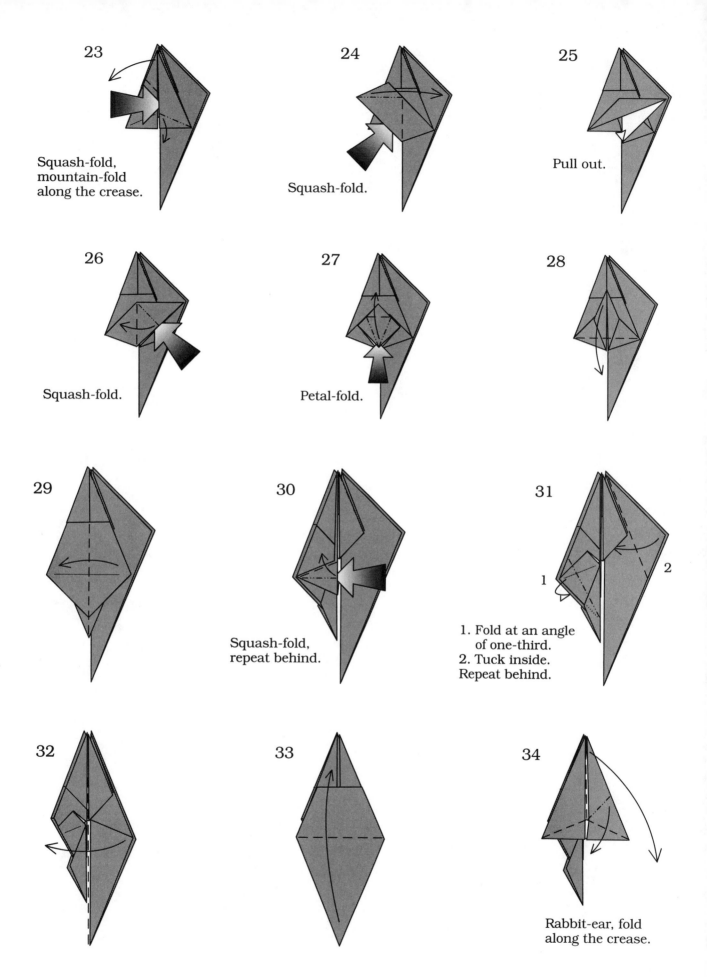

23

Squash-fold,
mountain-fold
along the crease.

24

Squash-fold.

25

Pull out.

26

Squash-fold.

27

Petal-fold.

28

29

30

Squash-fold,
repeat behind.

31

1
2

1. Fold at an angle
of one-third.
2. Tuck inside.
Repeat behind.

32

33

34

Rabbit-ear, fold
along the crease.

Rooster 59

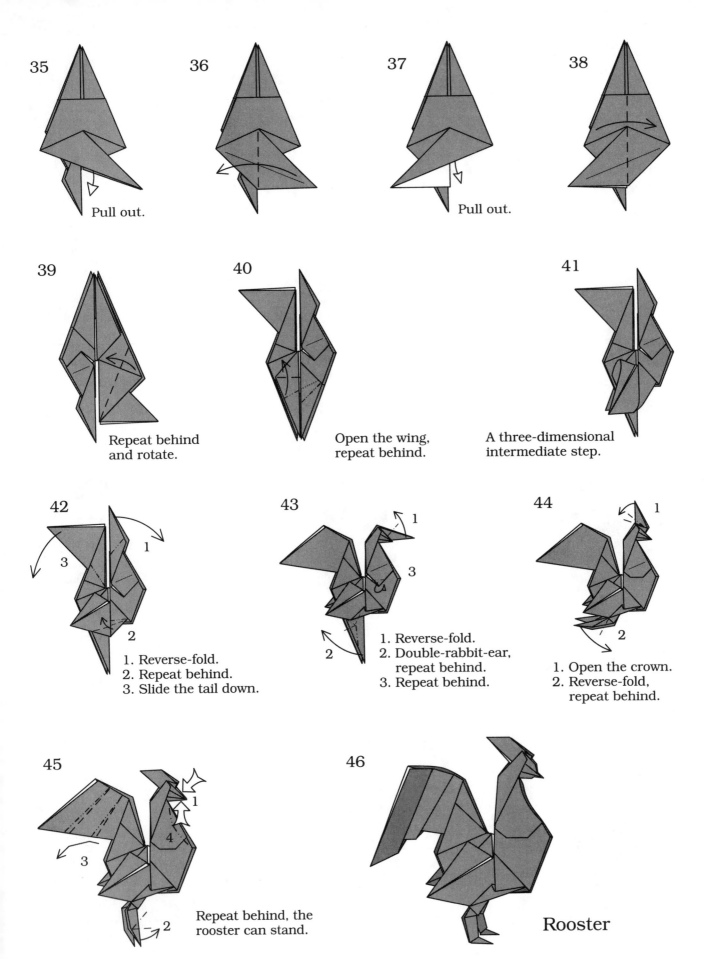

35

Pull out.

36

37

Pull out.

38

39

Repeat behind
and rotate.

40

Open the wing,
repeat behind.

41

A three-dimensional
intermediate step.

42

1
3
2

1. Reverse-fold.
2. Repeat behind.
3. Slide the tail down.

43

1
3
2

1. Reverse-fold.
2. Double-rabbit-ear,
   repeat behind.
3. Repeat behind.

44

1
2

1. Open the crown.
2. Reverse-fold,
   repeat behind.

45

1
4
3
2

Repeat behind, the
rooster can stand.

46

Rooster

Dog

Dog

犬

Chinese   Japanese
             "Inu"
  ˇ
"Quan"

い   ぬ

Year of the Dog

戌

Chinese   Japanese
 "Xū"   "Inu"

い   ぬ

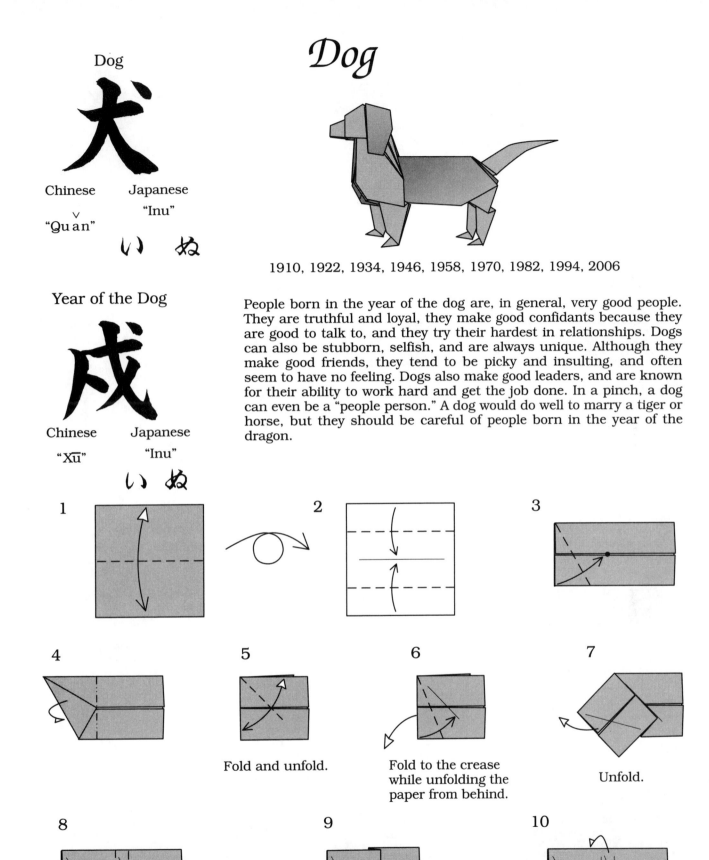

1910, 1922, 1934, 1946, 1958, 1970, 1982, 1994, 2006

People born in the year of the dog are, in general, very good people. They are truthful and loyal, they make good confidants because they are good to talk to, and they try their hardest in relationships. Dogs can also be stubborn, selfish, and are always unique. Although they make good friends, they tend to be picky and insulting, and often seem to have no feeling. Dogs also make good leaders, and are known for their ability to work hard and get the job done. In a pinch, a dog can even be a "people person." A dog would do well to marry a tiger or horse, but they should be careful of people born in the year of the dragon.

1

2

3

4

5

Fold and unfold.

6

Fold to the crease while unfolding the paper from behind.

7

Unfold.

8

9

Unfold.

10

11

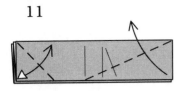

Repeat behind.

12

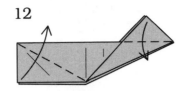

Repeat behind.

13

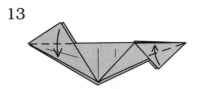

Repeat behind.

14

Unfold, repeat behind.

15

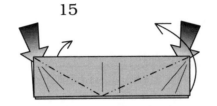

Reverse folds,
repeat behind.

16

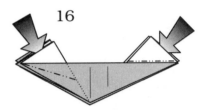

Reverse folds,
repeat behind.

17

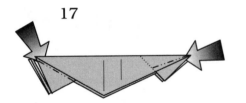

Reverse folds,
repeat behind.

18

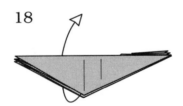

Open.

19

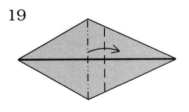

20

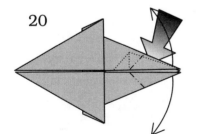

Reverse folds.

21

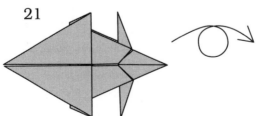

22

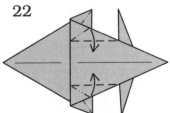

Squash folds.

23

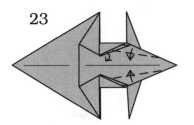

Slide out.

24

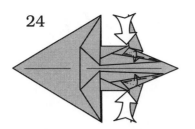

Spread squash folds.

25

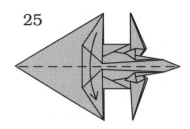

26

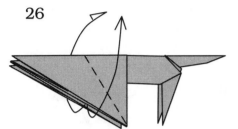

Outside-reverse-fold.

27

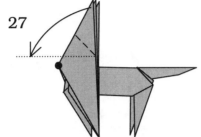

Outside-reverse-fold
above the dot.

28

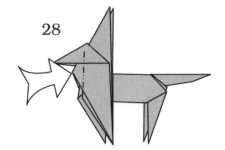

Sink.

29

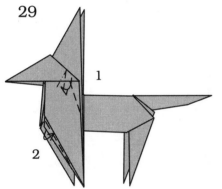

Repeat behind.

30

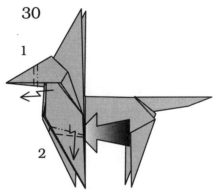

Crimp folds, repeat behind.

31

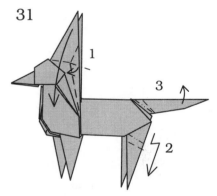

Crimp-fold the hind legs
and tail. Repeat behind.

32

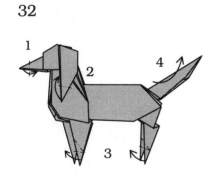

Reverse-fold the head and ears,
crimp-fold the feet and curl the
tail. Repeat behind.

33

Dog

Boar

1911, 1923, 1935, 1947, 1959, 1971, 1983, 1995, 2007

The year of the boar tends to make those born in it gallant, brave, and ambitious. Boars are honest, but do not say much, when they do talk. It is no use trying to stop them until they are finished, because boars will speak their minds. Boars are very determined, and when they do something, they put their whole heart into it. Boars are like monkeys in that they want to learn, and while they appear to be very knowledgeable they are not. They are full of trivial facts, but their knowledge does not run as deep as a monkey's. They make up for it though, in their kindness and affection. They have a temper, but tend avoid arguing. Boars should steer clear of the snake, but boars do form good relationships with rabbits and rams.

Boar

Chinese   Japanese

"Zhū"   "Inoshishi"

いのしし

Year of the Boar

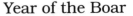

Chinese   Japanese

"Hài"   "I"

い

1
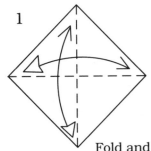
Fold and unfold along the diagonals.

2
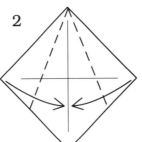

3
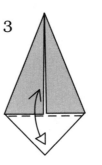
Fold and unfold.

4
Fold and unfold.

5
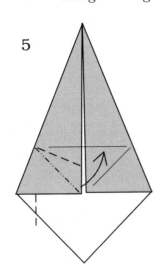
Squash-fold.

6
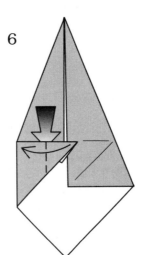
Squash-fold.

7
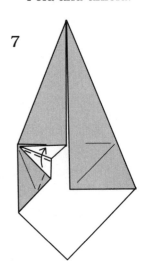
Squash-fold.

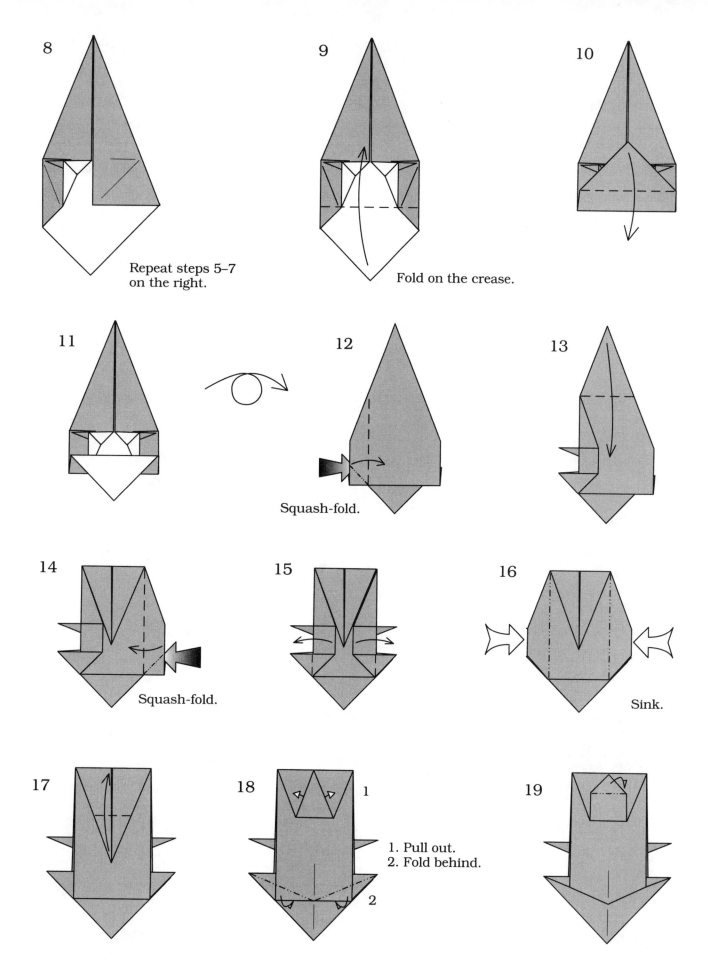

8

Repeat steps 5–7
on the right.

9

Fold on the crease.

10

11

12

Squash-fold.

13

14

Squash-fold.

15

16

Sink.

17

18

1. Pull out.
2. Fold behind.

1

2

19

Boar 65

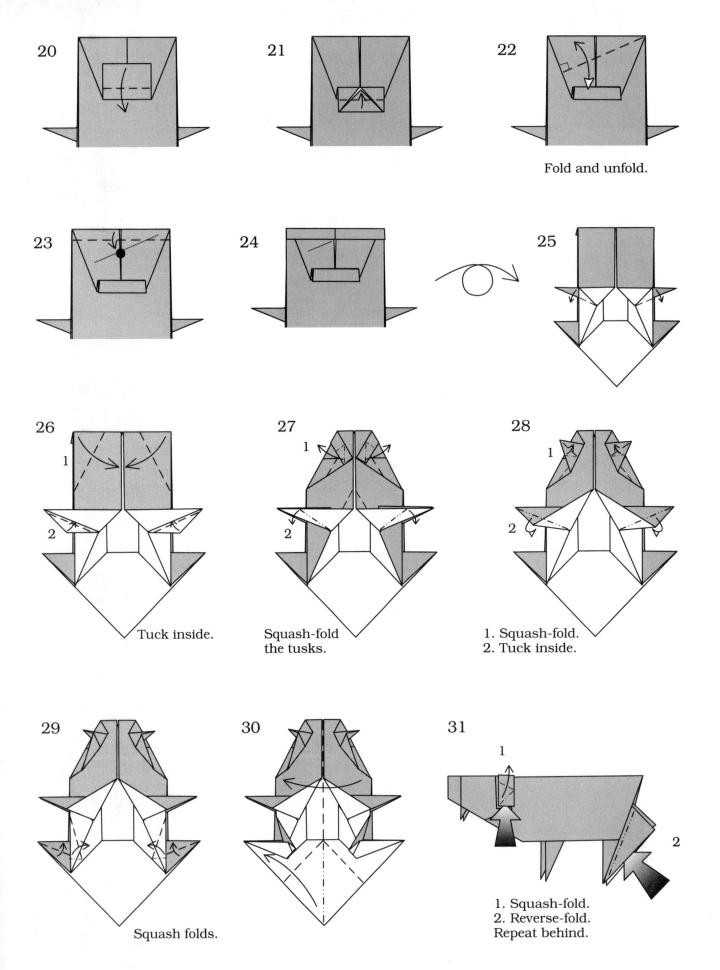

20

21

22

Fold and unfold.

23

24

25

26

Tuck inside.

27

Squash-fold
the tusks.

28

1. Squash-fold.
2. Tuck inside.

29

Squash folds.

30

31

1. Squash-fold.
2. Reverse-fold.
Repeat behind.

32

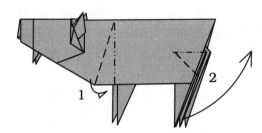

Crimp folds.

33

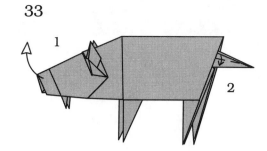

1. Unfold the crimp.
2. Repeat behind.

34

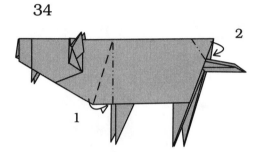

1. Tuck inside the pocket
   for the crimp fold.
2. Reverse-fold.

35

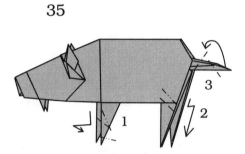

Crimp-fold the legs, reverse-fold
the tail, repeat behind.

36

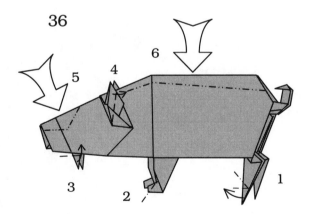

Repeat behind.

37

Boar

Mythological Creatures

Sea Serpent

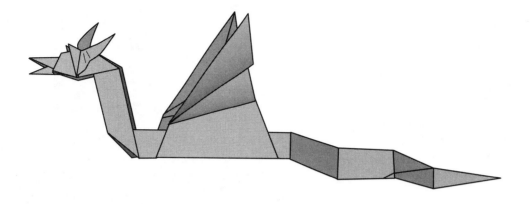

Sea serpents are essentially western dragons for sailors. Sailors were very superstitious, and if they came across a stretch of water they did not like, would draw sea serpents on their map and write "here be dragons." Sea serpents might actually be rooted in fact, like mermaids (which were thought to be the result of a very imaginative sailor's account of a manatee). Perhaps a sailor saw the tentacle of a giant squid or octopus and thought it was a sea serpent. Legends of sea serpents still exist today such as those of the Loch Ness Monster in Scotland, and Champy, the monster said to live in Lake Champlain in the United States. Modern scientists are still trying to prove the existence of these creatures.

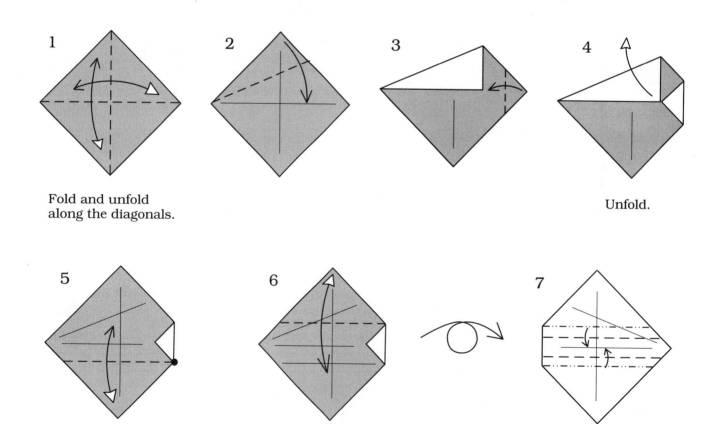

1
Fold and unfold
along the diagonals.

2

3

4
Unfold.

5
Fold up and unfold.

6
Fold and unfold.

7

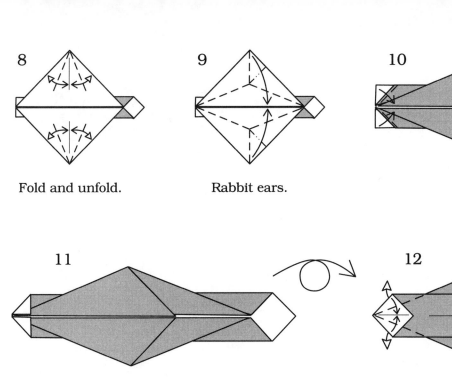

8

Fold and unfold.

9

Rabbit ears.

10

11

12

13

Unfold.

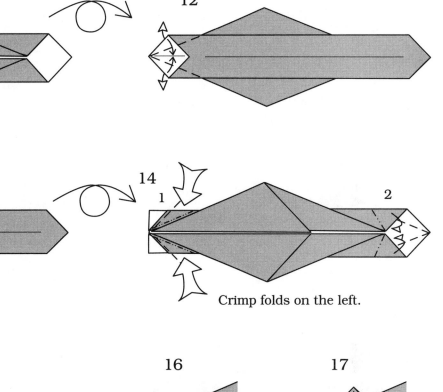

14

1

2

Crimp folds on the left.

15

Squash folds.

16

Pull out the white
paper from behind.

17

Fold and unfold.

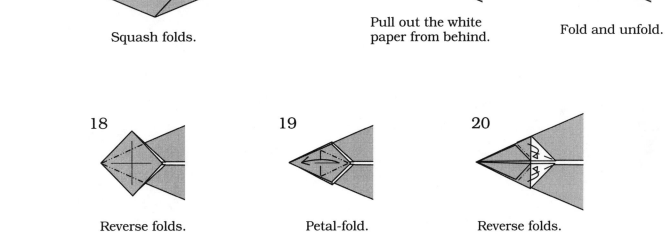

18

Reverse folds.

19

Petal-fold.

20

Reverse folds.

Sea Serpent 71

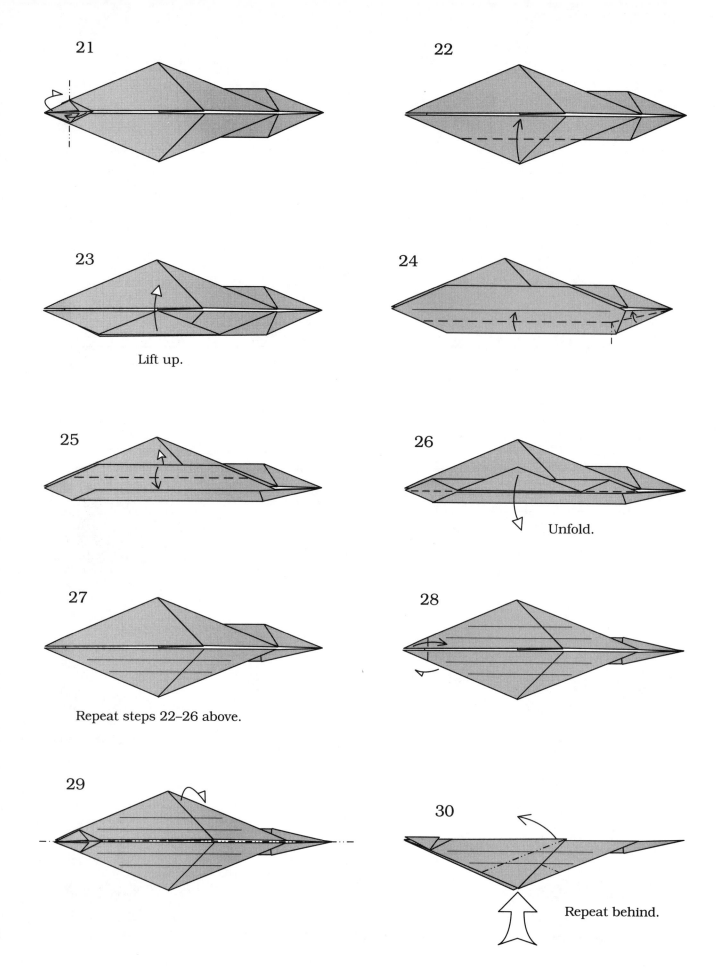

21

22

23

Lift up.

24

25

26

Unfold.

27

Repeat steps 22–26 above.

28

29

30

Repeat behind.

31

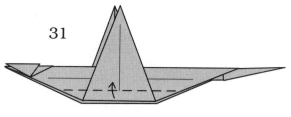

Repeat behind.

32

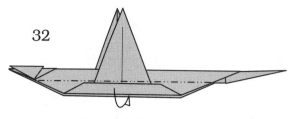

Repeat behind.

33

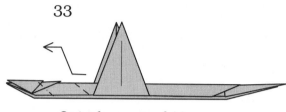

Outside reverse folds.

34

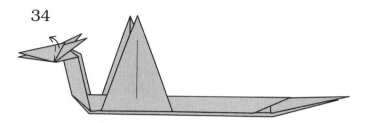

Repeat behind.

35

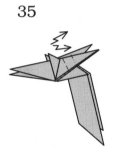

Repeat behind.

36

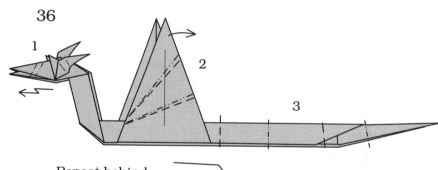

Repeat behind.

37

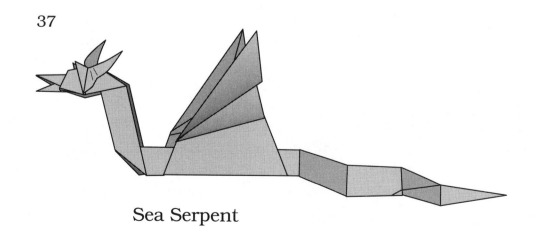

Sea Serpent

Unicorn

The unicorn is a legendary creature that resembles a pure white horse with a twisted horn coming out from its forehead. The horn is believed to have magic powers, especially for healing and is a symbol for purity and chastity. Sometimes the unicorn is pictured with a white lion's tail and the male may have a white beard, like a goat. The unicorn, like the griffin, was popular in medieval art.

1

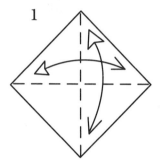

Fold and unfold.

2

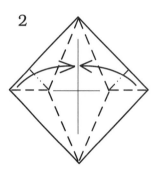

Rabbit ears.

3

Divide in thirds.

4

Fold to the bottom.

5

Fold and unfold.

6

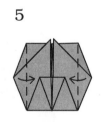

Unfold.

7

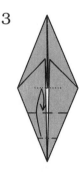

Sink.

8

9

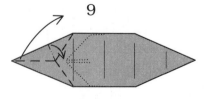

Rabbit-ear.

10

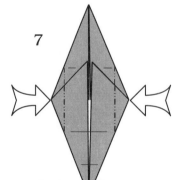

11

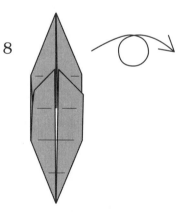

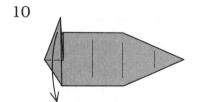

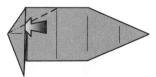

Reverse-fold.

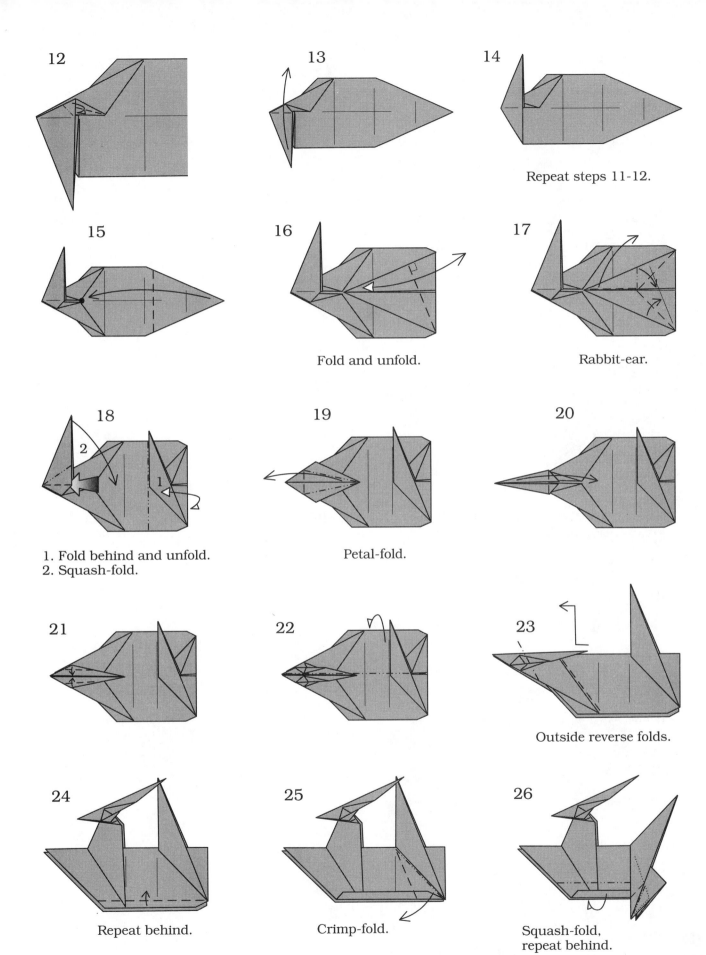

12

13

14

Repeat steps 11-12.

15

16

Fold and unfold.

17

Rabbit-ear.

18

1. Fold behind and unfold.
2. Squash-fold.

19

Petal-fold.

20

21

22

23

Outside reverse folds.

24

Repeat behind.

25

Crimp-fold.

26

Squash-fold,
repeat behind.

27

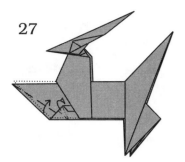

The underside layer is shown, fold at an angle of one-third. Repeat on the other leg.

28

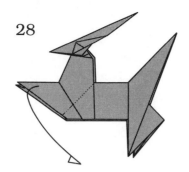

Repeat behind.

29

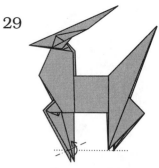

Reverse-fold, repeat behind.

30

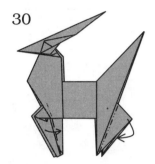

Reverse folds, repeat behind.

31

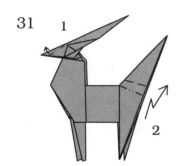

1. Spread the head, repeat behind.
2. Reverse folds.

32

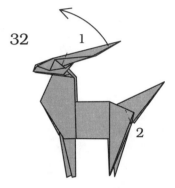

1. Outside-reverse-fold.
2. Reverse-fold, repeat behind.

33

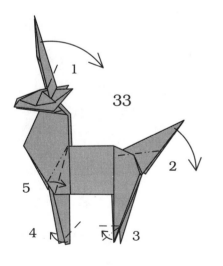

Repeat behind.

34

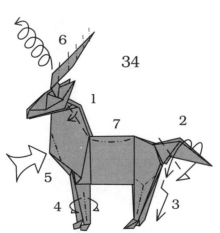

Repeat behind.

35

Unicorn

Centaur

Centaurs are a race of mythological creatures from ancient Greece. They had the upper body of a human, and the lower body of a horse. In general, centaurs were wild, clever, and savage. The constellation Sagittarius, which is Latin for archer, is a centaur.

1

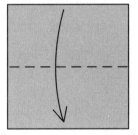

2

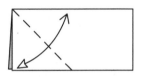

Fold and unfold.

3

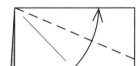

4

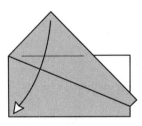

Unfold.

5

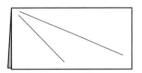

Repeat steps 2–4 on the right and behind.

6

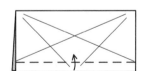

Repeat behind.

7

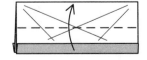

Repeat behind.

8

Fold and unfold, repeat behind.

9

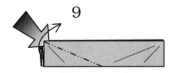

Reverse-fold, repeat behind.

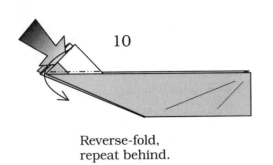

10

Reverse-fold,
repeat behind.

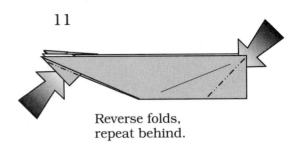

11

Reverse folds,
repeat behind.

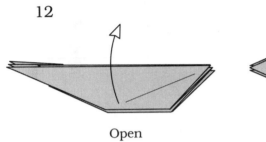

12

Open

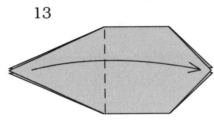

13

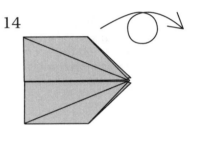

14

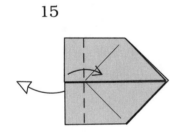

15

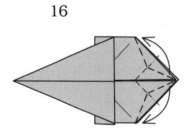

16

Rabbit ears.

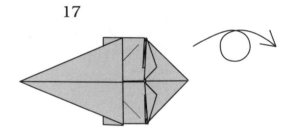

17

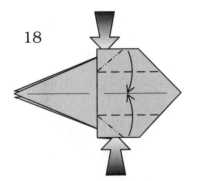

18

Squash-fold to the center line.

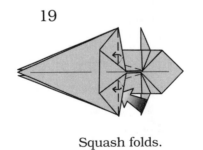

19

Squash folds.

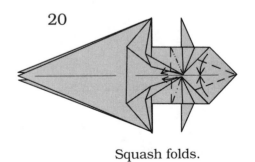

20

Squash folds.

21

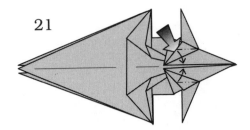

Unlock the paper.

22

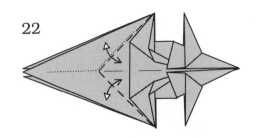

Fold and unfold.

23

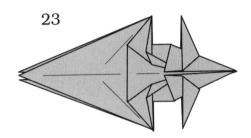

24

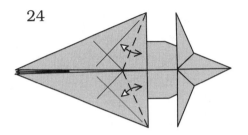

Fold and unfold.

25

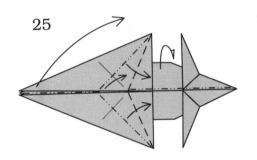

26

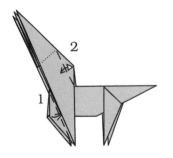

1. Tuck, repeat behind.
2. Fold and unfold.

27

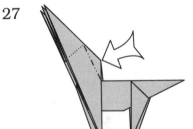

Sink.

28

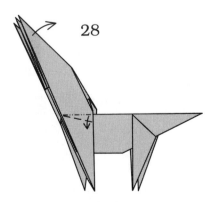

Crimp-fold.

29

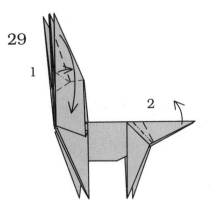

1. Repeat behind.
2. Crimp-fold.

30

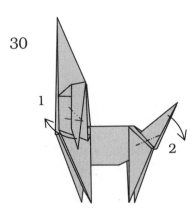

1. Crimp-fold, repeat behind.
2. Reverse-fold.

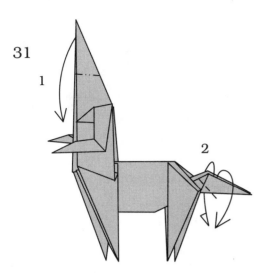

31

1

2

1. Reverse-fold.
2. Outside-reverse-fold.

32

Reverse folds.

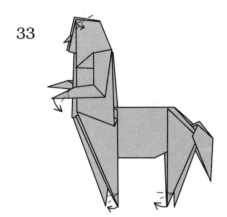

33

Fold the hands, hooves,
and eyes, repeat behind.

34

Crimp-fold at the head.
Repeat behind.

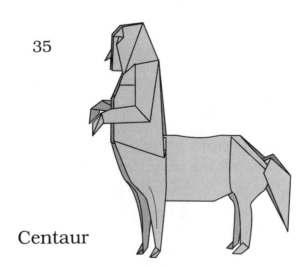

35

Centaur

Griffin

Griffins are mythical animals with the body of a lion and the wings, head, and neck of an eagle. Occasionally, they have the talons of an eagle, or the tail of a snake. Griffins were originally from the early Middle Eastern legends, but found their way into Roman and Christian cultures. Many gargoyles found on medieval churches are griffins, because the creatures represent strength and vigilance. For this reason they are also very common on coats of arms, and the symbol of the city of Perugia, in Italy, is the griffin. They are said to live in nests high up in the mountains, where they guard their ill-gotten hoards of gold from human plunderers.

1

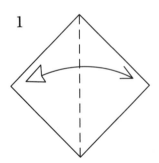

Fold and unfold along the diagonal.

2

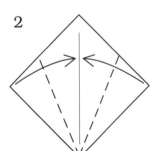

3

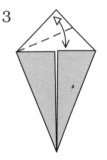

Fold and unfold.

4

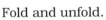

5

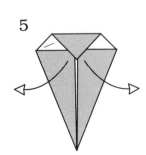

Unfold.

6

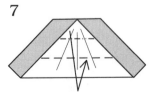

7

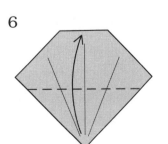

Fold in thirds.

8

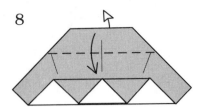

9

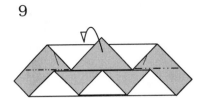

10

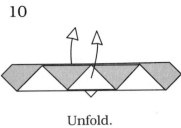

Unfold.

11

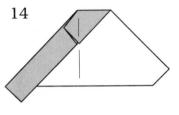

12

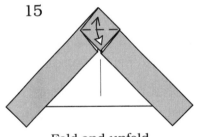

Squash-fold.

13

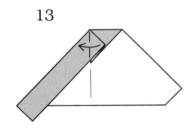

14

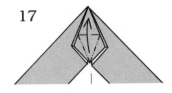

Repeat steps 12–13
on the right.

15

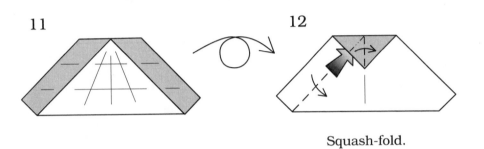

Fold and unfold.

16

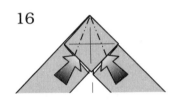

Reverse folds.

17

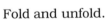

Petal-fold.

18

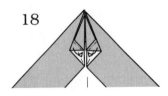

Reverse folds.

19

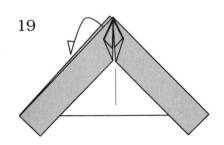

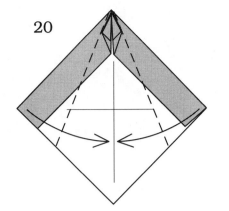

20

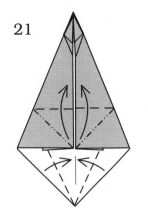

21

Squash folds.

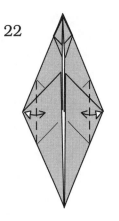

22

Fold and unfold.

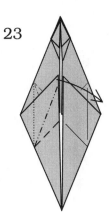

23

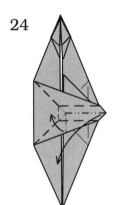

24

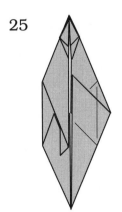

25

Repeat steps 23–24
on the right.

26

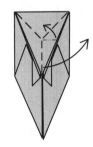

27

Rabbit-ear.

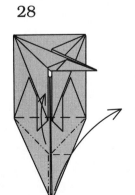

28

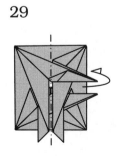

29

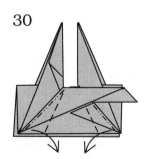

30

Crimp folds.

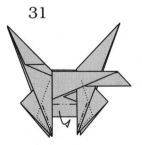

31

Thin the legs from behind
while thinning the body,
repeat behind.

32

Reverse folds,

33

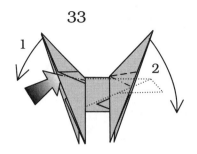

1. Reverse-fold.
2. Crimp-fold.

34

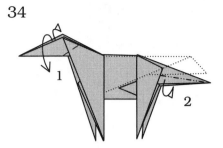

1. Outside-reverse-fold.
2. Repeat behind.

35

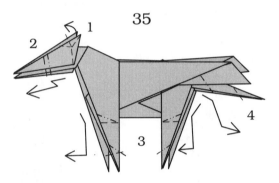

1. Rabbit-ear.
2. Crimp-fold.
3, 4. Shape the legs and tail.
Repeat behind.

36

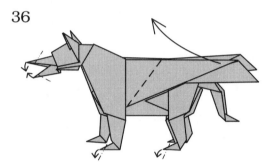

Repeat behind.

37

Griffin

Pegasus

Pegasus was the Greek mythological winged horse. He was white and had feathered wings, like those of a bird. Pegasus sprang out of the neck of Medusa, the hideous monster who, when seen, turned people into stone, when Perseus cut her head off. From there, he flew to Greece, and the nine muses, minor goddesses who were patrons of the arts, took care of him. Pegasus was a wild horse, and no one but the muses could go near him. Athena, the goddess after whom Athens was named, gave Bellerophon, the great horse tamer, a golden bridle with which to tame Pegasus. Bellerophon managed to slip the bridle onto Pegasus to kill the Chimera, and then, being arrogant and overconfident, used Pegasus to fly up to Olympus, the home of the gods, uninvited. Zeus, the chief Greek god, sent out a fly, which made Pegasus buck, and Bellerophon fell. After that, Pegasus was used by Zeus to carry his thunderbolts, his favorite weapons.

1
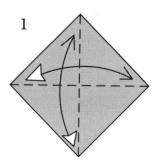

Fold and unfold along the diagonals.

2
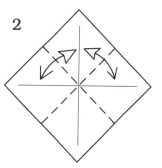

Fold and unfold.

3
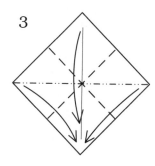

Collapse the square by bringing the four corners together.

4
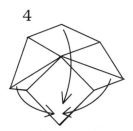

This is a three-dimensional intermediate step.

5

Repeat behind.

6
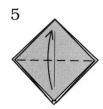

Unfold, repeat behind.

7
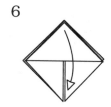

Fold and unfold, repeat behind.

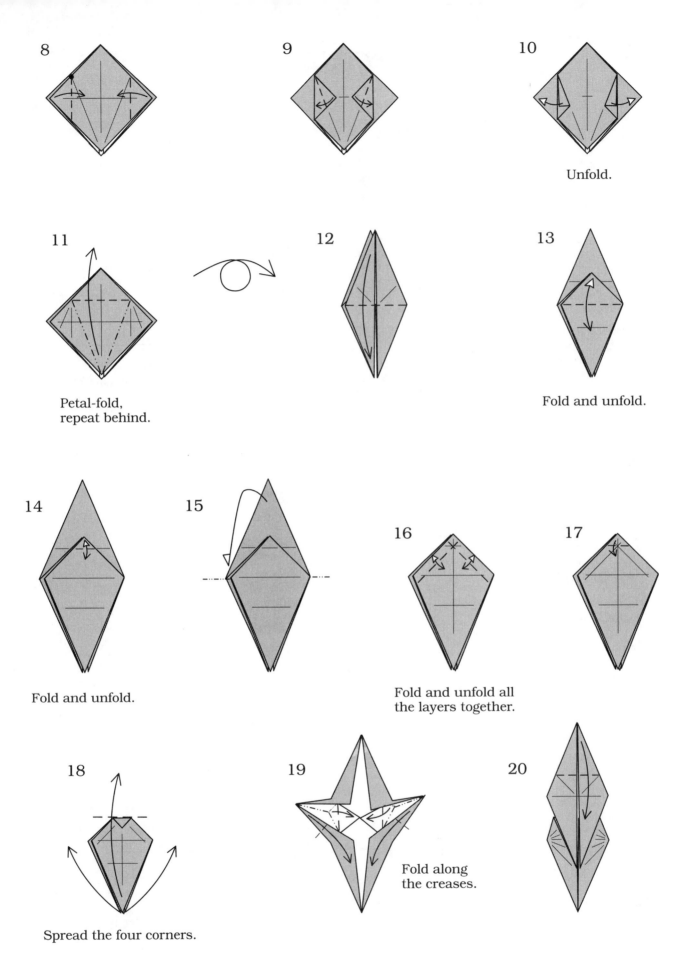

8

9

10

Unfold.

11

Petal-fold,
repeat behind.

12

13

Fold and unfold.

14

Fold and unfold.

15

16

17

Fold and unfold all
the layers together.

18

Spread the four corners.

19

Fold along
the creases.

20

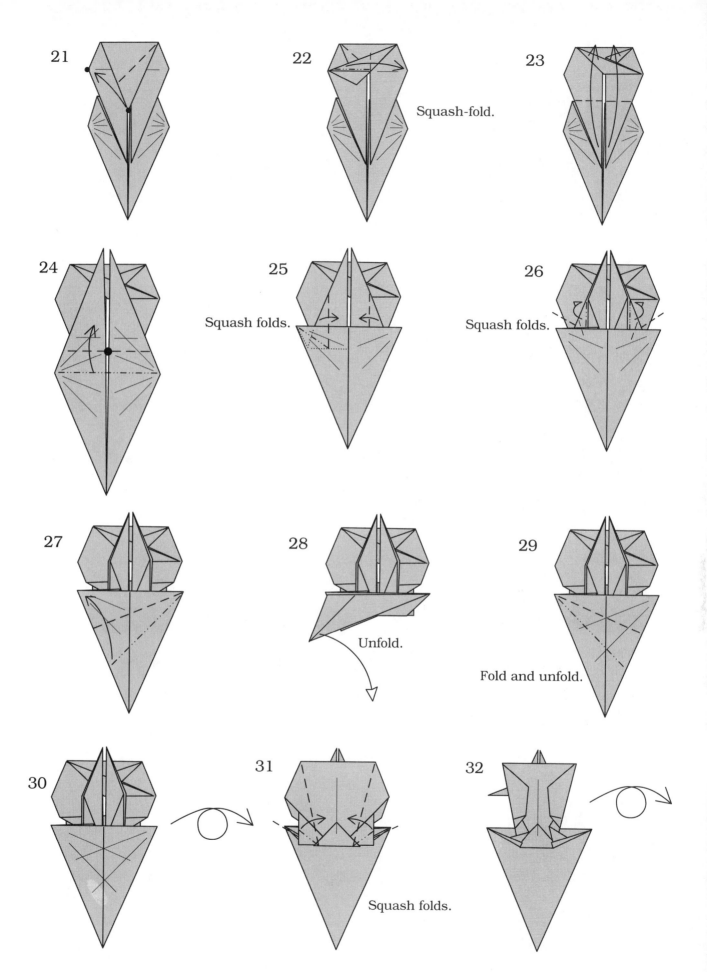

21

22 Squash-fold.

23

24

25 Squash folds.

26 Squash folds.

27

28 Unfold.

29 Fold and unfold.

30

31 Squash folds.

32

Pegasus 87

33

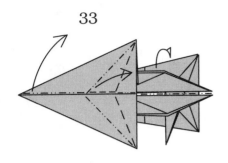

34

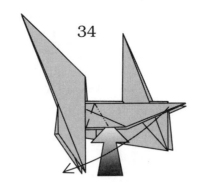

Squash-fold,
repeat behind.

35

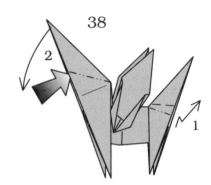

1. Crimp-fold.
2. Petal-fold,
   repeat behind.

36

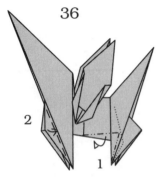

1. Thin the leg and body.
2. Tuck inside.
Repeat behind.

37

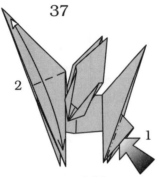

1. Reverse-fold.
2. Fold to the bottom
   and unfold.

38

1. Crimp-fold.
2. Reverse-fold.

39

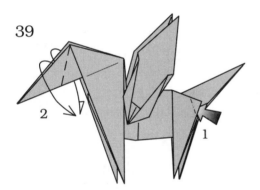

1. Reverse-fold, repeat behind.
2. Outside-reverse-fold.

40

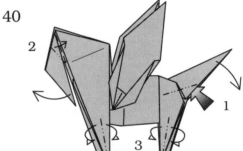

1. Reverse-fold.
2. Crimp-fold.
3. Thin the legs,
   repeat behind.

41

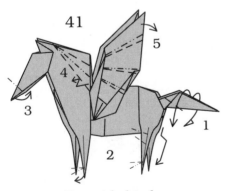

Repeat behind.

42

Pegasus

Cerberus

In Greek mythology, Cerberus is the three-headed dog that guards the gate to the underworld, letting everyone in, but no one out. He is the child of the half-woman, half-monster Echidne, who was also the mother of Ladon the dragon, Orthrus the two-headed dog, the Lernan Hydra, the Chimera, the Sphinx, and the Nemean Lion. His father was the hundred headed monster Typhon. It is said that where Cerberus' saliva falls, the poisonous plant wolf's bane grows.

1

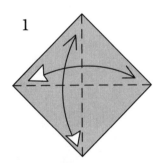

Fold and unfold
along the diagonals.

2

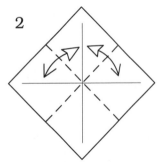

Fold and unfold.

3

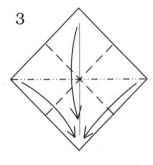

Collapse the square
by bringing the four
corners together.

4

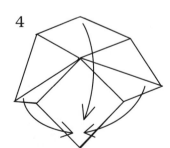

This is a three-
dimensional
intermediate step.

5

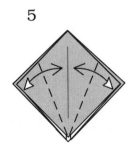

Fold and unfold,
repeat behind.

6

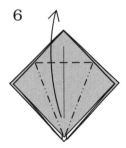

Petal-fold,
repeat behind.

7

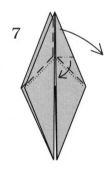

Rabbit-ear.

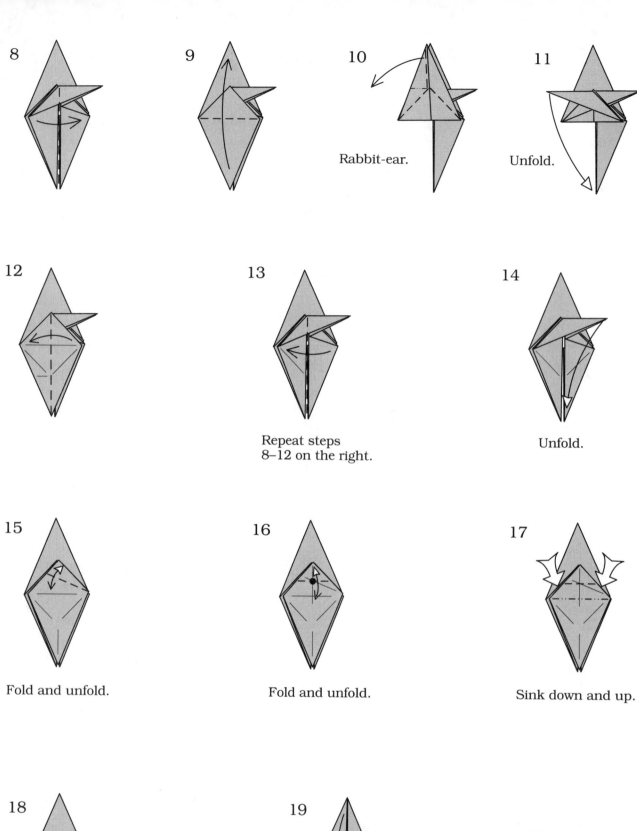

8

9

10

Rabbit-ear.

11

Unfold.

12

13

Repeat steps
8–12 on the right.

14

Unfold.

15

Fold and unfold.

16

Fold and unfold.

17

Sink down and up.

18

19

20

Rabbit-ear.

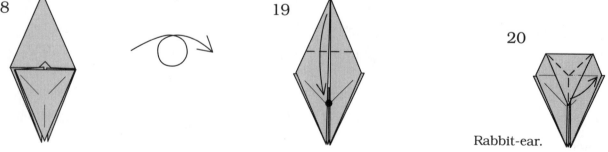

21

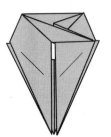

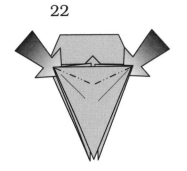

22

Reverse folds.

23

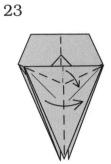

24

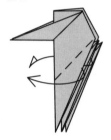

Outside-reverse-fold.

25

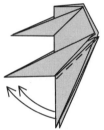

Outside-reverse-folds
and rotate.

26

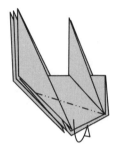

Repeat behind.

27

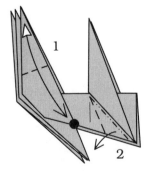

1. Fold and unfold.
2. Crimp-fold.

28

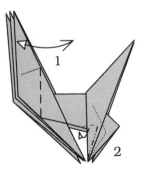

1. Fold and unfold.
2. Thin the leg and body,
   repeat behind.

29

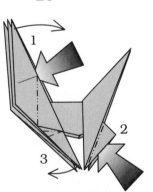

1. Reverse-fold.
2. Reverse-fold.
3. Crimp-fold.
Repeat behind.

30

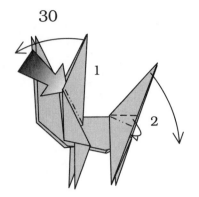

1. Reverse-fold.
2. Crimp-fold.

31

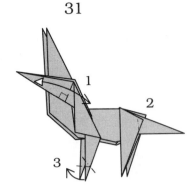

1. Fold and unfold.
2. Reverse-fold.
3. Crimp-fold.
Repeat behind.

32

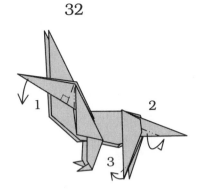

1. Crimp-fold.
2. Repeat behind.
3. Reverse-fold.
Repeat behind.

33

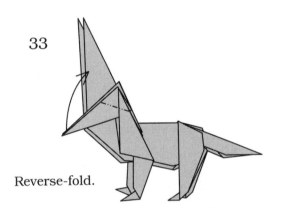

Reverse-fold.

34

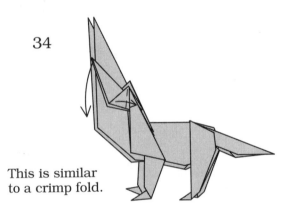

This is similar
to a crimp fold.

35

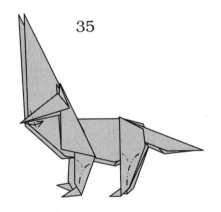

Reverse-fold the tip of the head, fold
the two remaining heads beginning
with step 27 though the heads could
be different, shape the legs.

36

Cerberus

Wyvern

The wyvern is a mythical medieval creature that resembles a small dragon. Wyverns have two legs, and are often depicted as being half dragon and half bird. They are often found on medieval, and some modern, coats of arms.

1

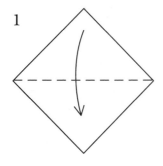

2

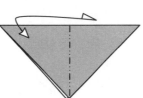

Fold behind
and unfold.

3

Fold one layer up
and unfold.

4

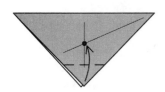

5

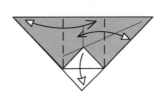

Fold and unfold.

6

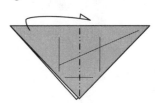

7

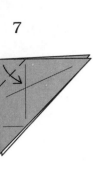

8

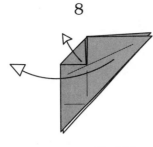

Unfold.

9

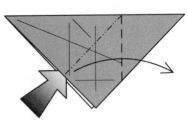

Squash-fold.

10

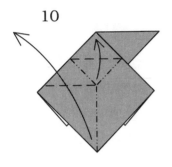

11

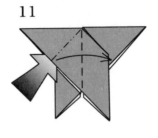

Squash-fold,
repeat behind.

12

Fold and unfold,
repeat behind.

13

Reverse folds,
repeat behind.

14

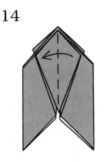

Repeat behind.

15

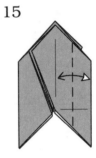

Fold and unfold, repeat
on the other side.

16

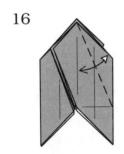

Fold and unfold, repeat
on the other side.

17

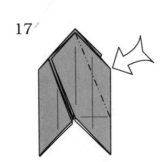

Sink, repeat on
the other side.

18

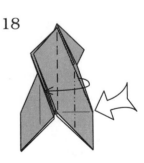

Spread-squash-fold,
repeat on the other side.

19

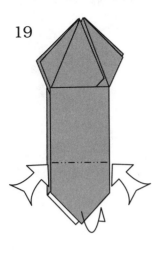

Reverse-fold inside along the crease. If the crease is not on this side then turn over.

20

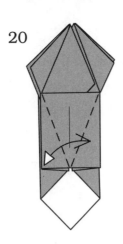

Fold and unfold.

21

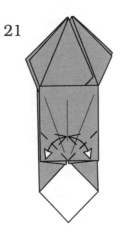

Fold and unfold.

22

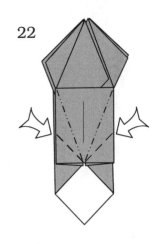

Crimp folds.

23

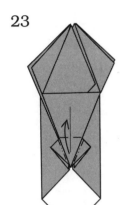

Petal-fold.

24

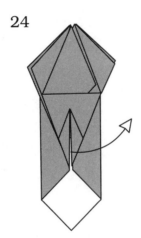

Pull out the hidden corner.

25

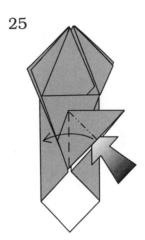

Squash-fold.

26

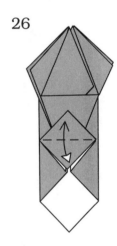

Fold and unfold.

27

Reverse folds.

28

Petal-fold.

29

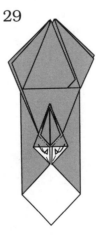

Reverse folds.

30

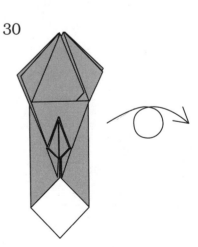

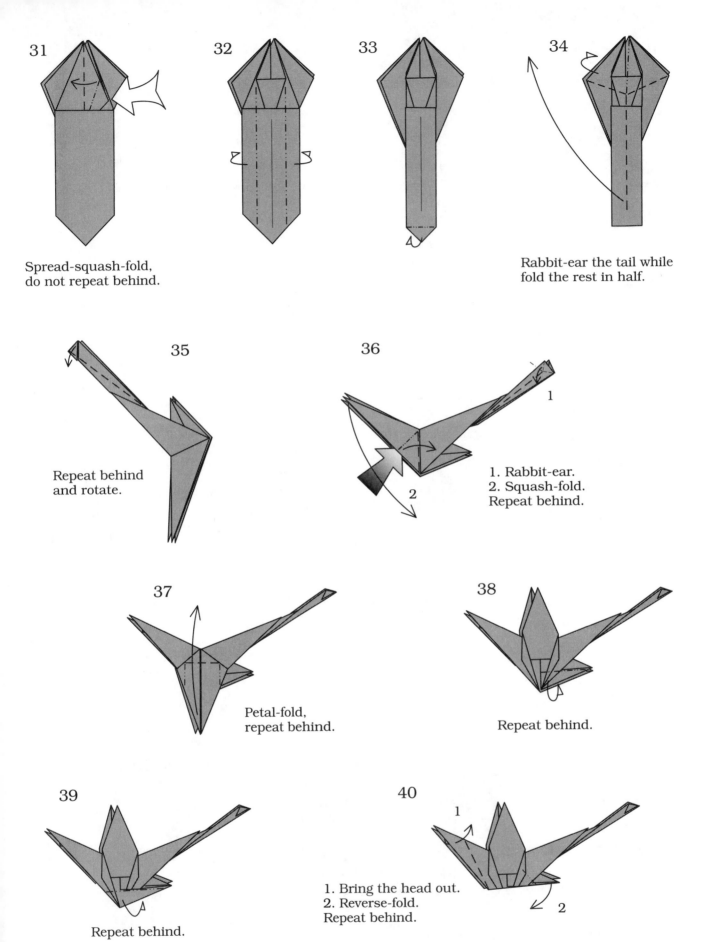

31

Spread-squash-fold,
do not repeat behind.

32

33

34

Rabbit-ear the tail while
fold the rest in half.

35

Repeat behind
and rotate.

36

1

2

1. Rabbit-ear.
2. Squash-fold.
Repeat behind.

37

Petal-fold,
repeat behind.

38

Repeat behind.

39

Repeat behind.

40

1

2

1. Bring the head out.
2. Reverse-fold.
Repeat behind.

41

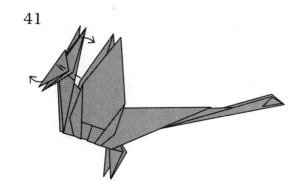

42

Repeat behind.

43

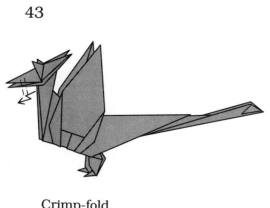

Crimp-fold.

44

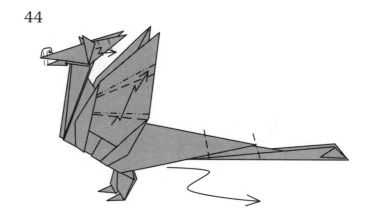

Repeat behind, curl the tail.

45

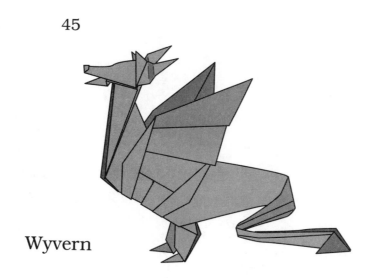

Wyvern

Western Dragon

The Western dragon is virtually the opposite of the Chinese dragon. The Western dragon is shorter than its Chinese conterpart, and is generally considered bad, while Chinese dragons are good and wise. Western dragons are usually green and have wings for flight. Chinese dragons are often red, and require no wings to fly. Western dragons are very popular in fairy tales, where the brave knights save beautiful damsels in distress from them. A very famous knight who killed a dragon is Saint George.

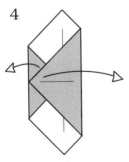

1

Fold and unfold
along the diagonals.

2

3

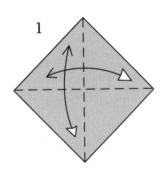

4

Unfold.

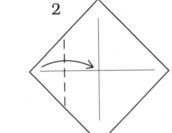

5

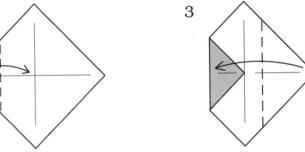

6

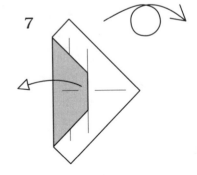

7

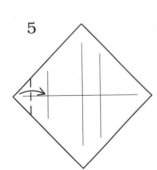

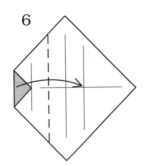

Unfold.

8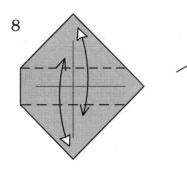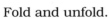

Fold and unfold.

9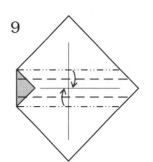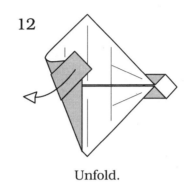

10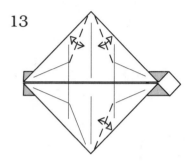

Fold and unfold.

11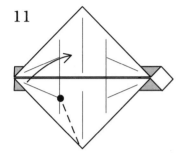

12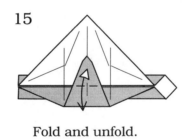

Unfold.

13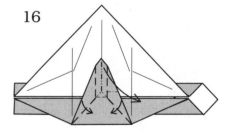

Fold and unfold.

14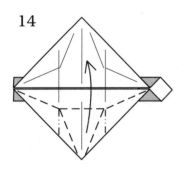

15

Fold and unfold.

16

17

Repeat steps 14–16 above.

18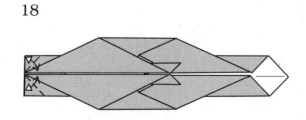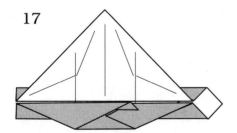

Fold and unfold.

Western Dragon 99

19

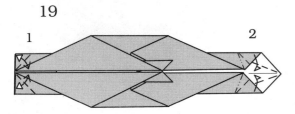

20

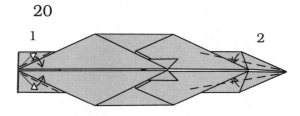

1. Fold and unfold.
2. Fold inside.

21

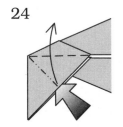

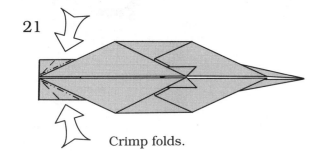

Crimp folds.

22

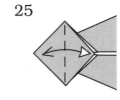

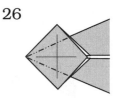

Squash folds.

23

Pull out the hidden, original corner of the square.

24

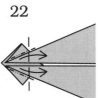

Squash-fold.

25

Fold and unfold.

26

Reverse folds.

27

Petal-fold.

28

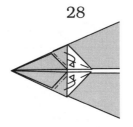

Reverse folds.

29

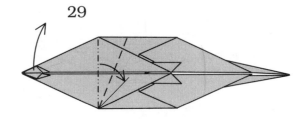

30

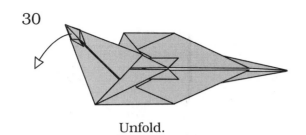

Unfold.

31

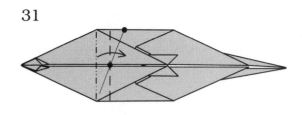

32

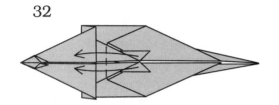

33

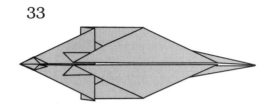

Repeat steps 29–31
on the right.

34

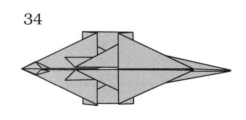

35

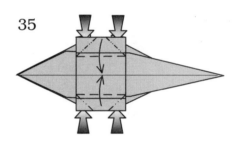

Squash-fold to the center.

36

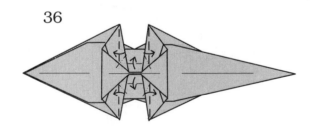

37

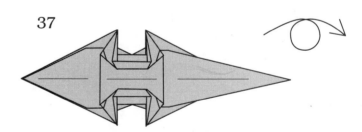

38

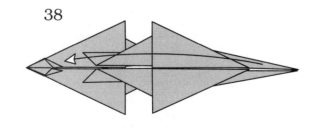

39

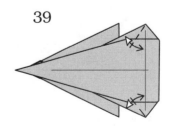

Fold and unfold.

40

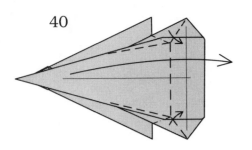

41

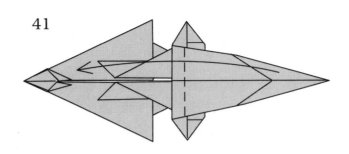

42

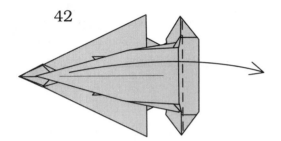

43

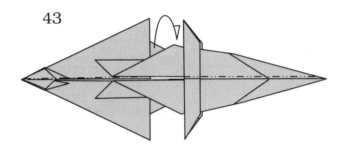

44

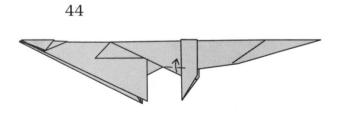

Repeat behind.

45

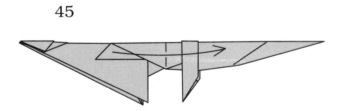

Repeat behind.

46

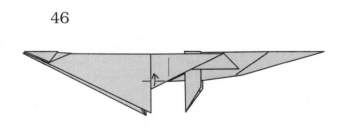

Repeat behind.

47

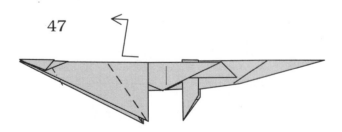

Outside reverse folds.

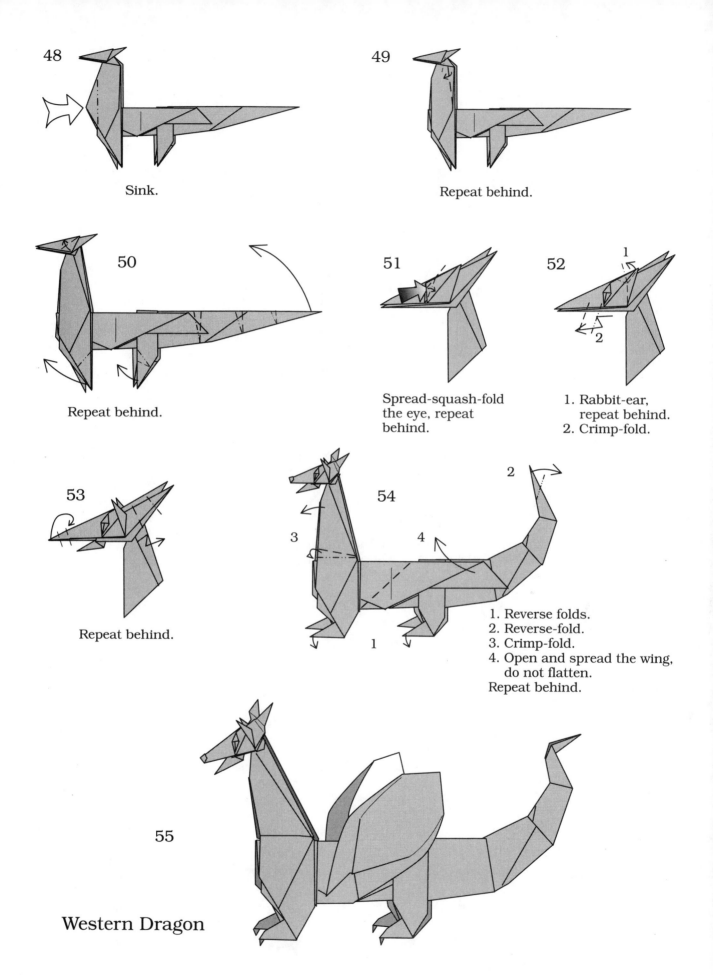

48

Sink.

49

Repeat behind.

50

Repeat behind.

51

Spread-squash-fold
the eye, repeat
behind.

52

1. Rabbit-ear,
   repeat behind.
2. Crimp-fold.

53

Repeat behind.

54

1. Reverse folds.
2. Reverse-fold.
3. Crimp-fold.
4. Open and spread the wing,
   do not flatten.
Repeat behind.

55

Western Dragon

Chimera

The Chimera was a fire-breathing three headed monster from ancient Greek mythology. It had one head of a lion, the body and another head of a goat, and either a snake tail or another head of a snake. The Chimera was the brother of Cerberus. It lived in Lycia, in Asia Minor and wreaked havoc on the people. Bellerophon, rider of Pegasus, had to kill the Chimera as a penance for killing his brother in a hunting accident. Astride Pegasus, Bellerophon flew over the Chimera and stuck a lance with a lump of lead on the end down the Chimera's throat. When the Chimera breathed fire at Bellerophon, the lead melted into Chimera's stomach and killed it. In literature, the Chimera has been used to represent that which is elusive and just out of reach.

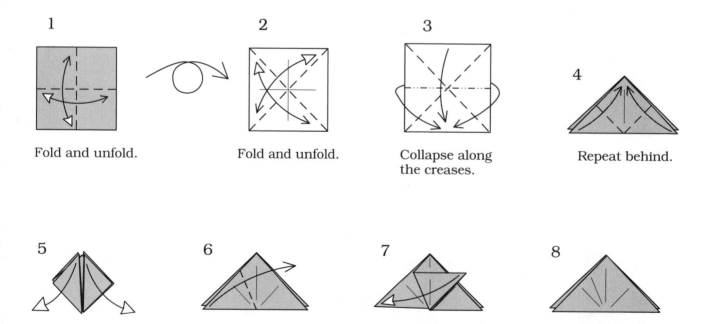

1

Fold and unfold.

2

Fold and unfold.

3

Collapse along the creases.

4

Repeat behind.

5

Unfold.

6

7

Unfold.

8

Repeat steps 6–7 on the right and behind.

9

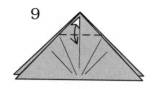

Fold down
and unfold.

10

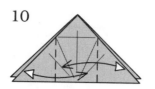

Fold and unfold,
repeat behind.

11

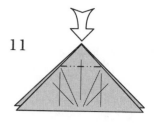

Begin the sink fold.

12

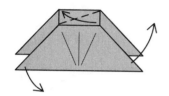

13

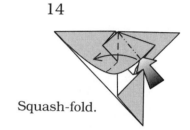

14

Squash-fold.

15

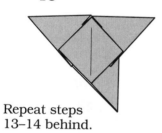

Repeat steps
13–14 behind.

16

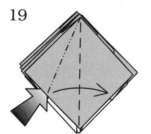

Squash-fold,
repeat behind.

17

18

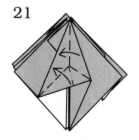

19

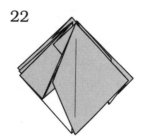

Squash-fold.

20

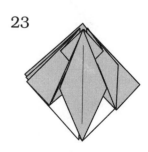

21

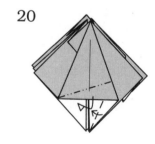

22

Repeat steps 19–21
on the right.

23

Repeat steps
19–22 behind.

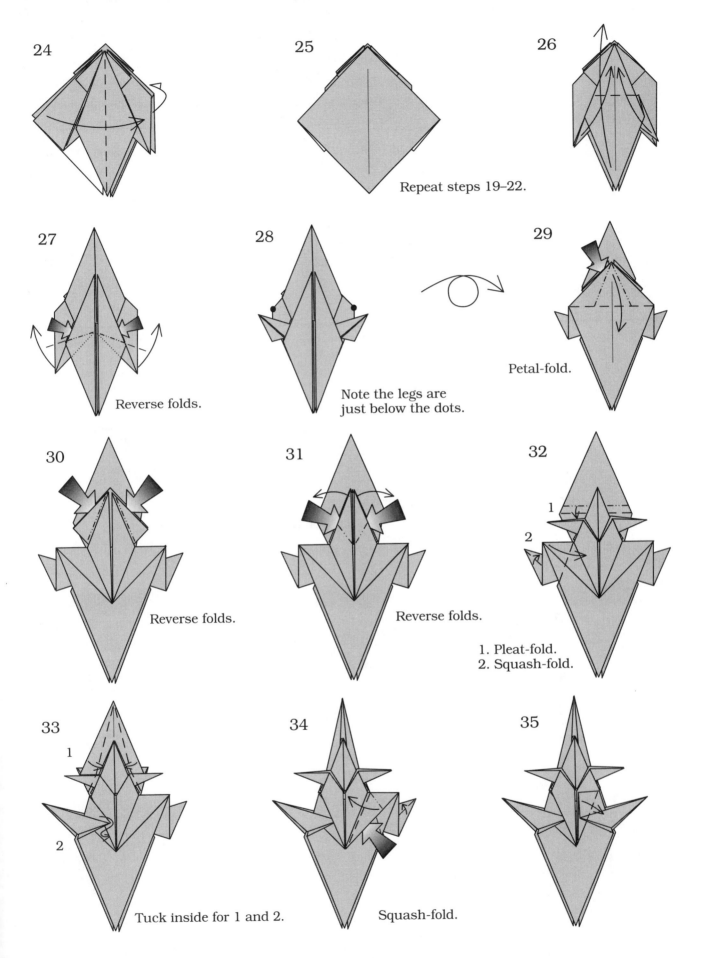

24

25

Repeat steps 19–22.

26

27

Reverse folds.

28

Note the legs are just below the dots.

29

Petal-fold.

30

Reverse folds.

31

Reverse folds.

32

1. Pleat-fold.
2. Squash-fold.

33

Tuck inside for 1 and 2.

34

Squash-fold.

35

36

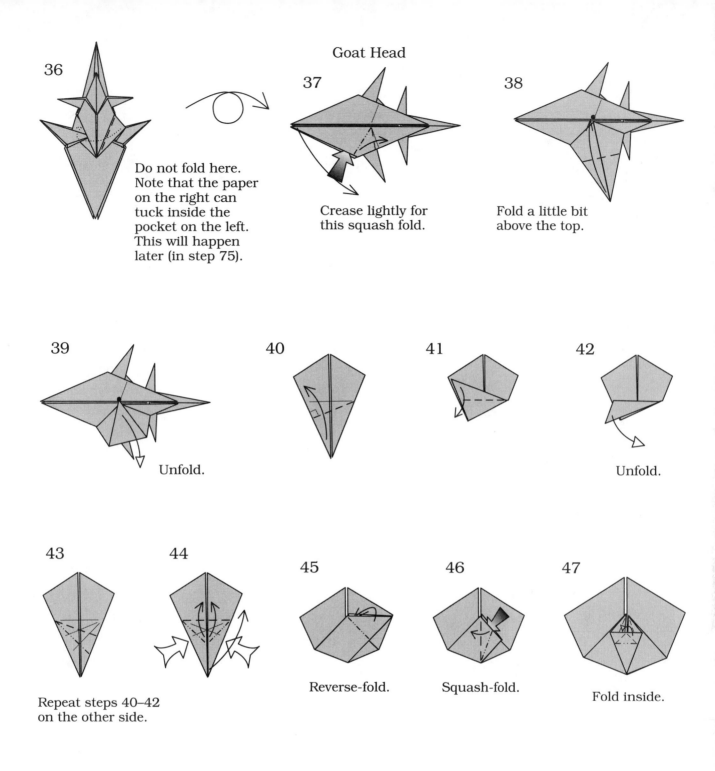

Do not fold here.
Note that the paper
on the right can
tuck inside the
pocket on the left.
This will happen
later (in step 75).

Goat Head

37

Crease lightly for
this squash fold.

38

Fold a little bit
above the top.

39

Unfold.

40

41

42

Unfold.

43

Repeat steps 40–42
on the other side.

44

45

Reverse-fold.

46

Squash-fold.

47

Fold inside.

48

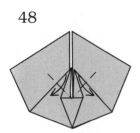

Reverse folds.

49

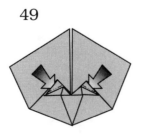

Reverse folds.

50

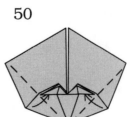

51

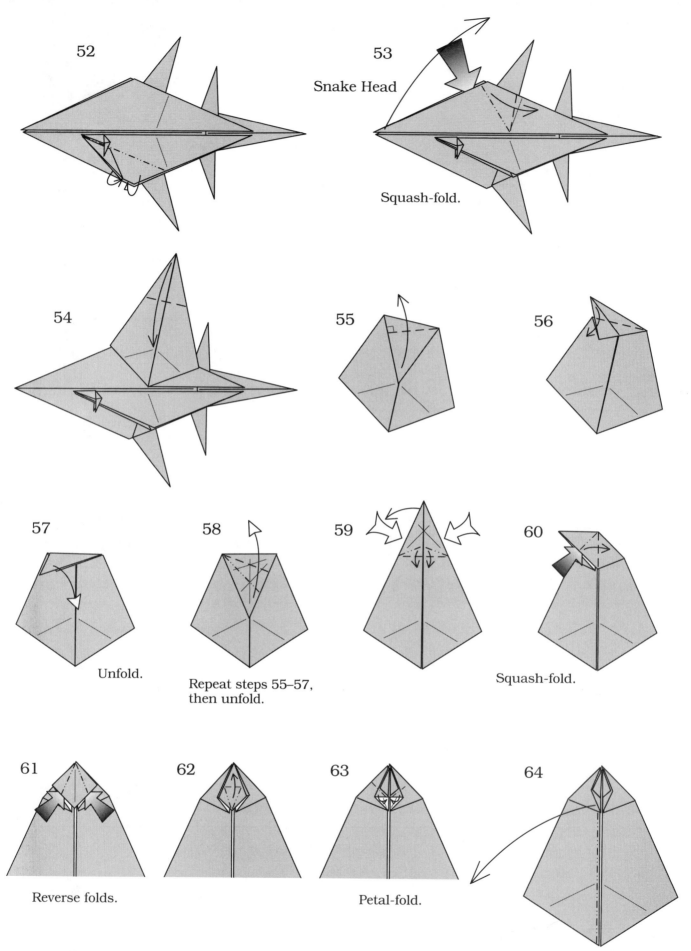

52

53

Snake Head

Squash-fold.

54

55

56

57

Unfold.

58

Repeat steps 55–57,
then unfold.

59

60

Squash-fold.

61

Reverse folds.

62

63

Petal-fold.

64

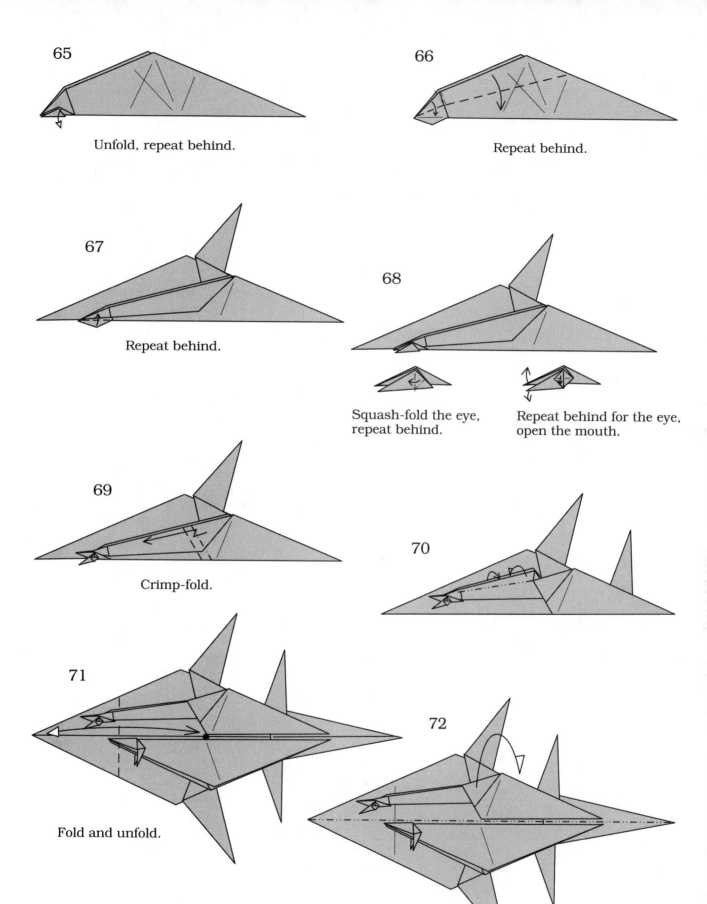

65

Unfold, repeat behind.

66

Repeat behind.

67

Repeat behind.

68

Squash-fold the eye, repeat behind.

Repeat behind for the eye, open the mouth.

69

Crimp-fold.

70

71

Fold and unfold.

72

73

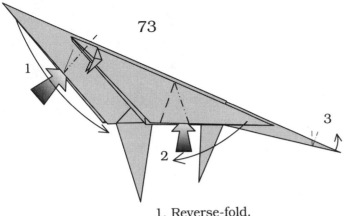

1. Reverse-fold.
2. Squash-fold, repeat behind.
3. Open the tip of the tail.

74

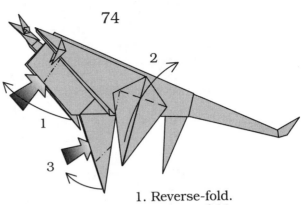

1. Reverse-fold.
2. Reverse-fold.
3. Squash-fold.
Repeat behind.

75

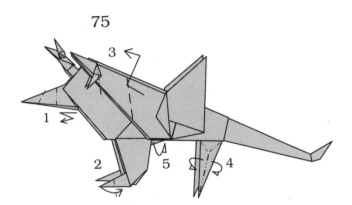

1. Reverse folds.
2. Reverse folds for the goat neck.
3. Reverse-fold, repeat behind.
4. Thin the legs, repeat behind.
5. Tuck inside the pocket to lock the model.

76

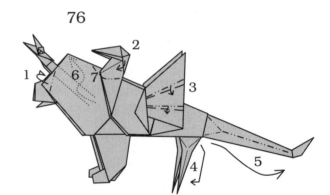

1. Repeat beind.
2. Curl the horns, repeat behind.
3. Pleat the wings, repeat behind.
4. Shape the legs, repeat behind.
5. Thin and curl the tail.
6. Curl the snake.
7. Round out the lion's mane.

77

Chimera

Three-Headed Dragon

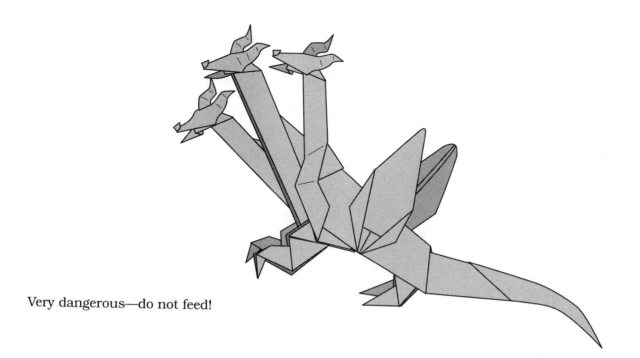

Very dangerous—do not feed!

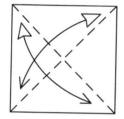

Fold and unfold.

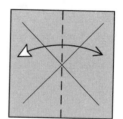

Fold and unfold.

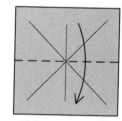

Fold to the dotted line.

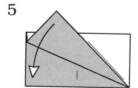

Unfold.

Fold and unfold.

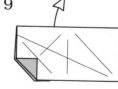

Unfold.

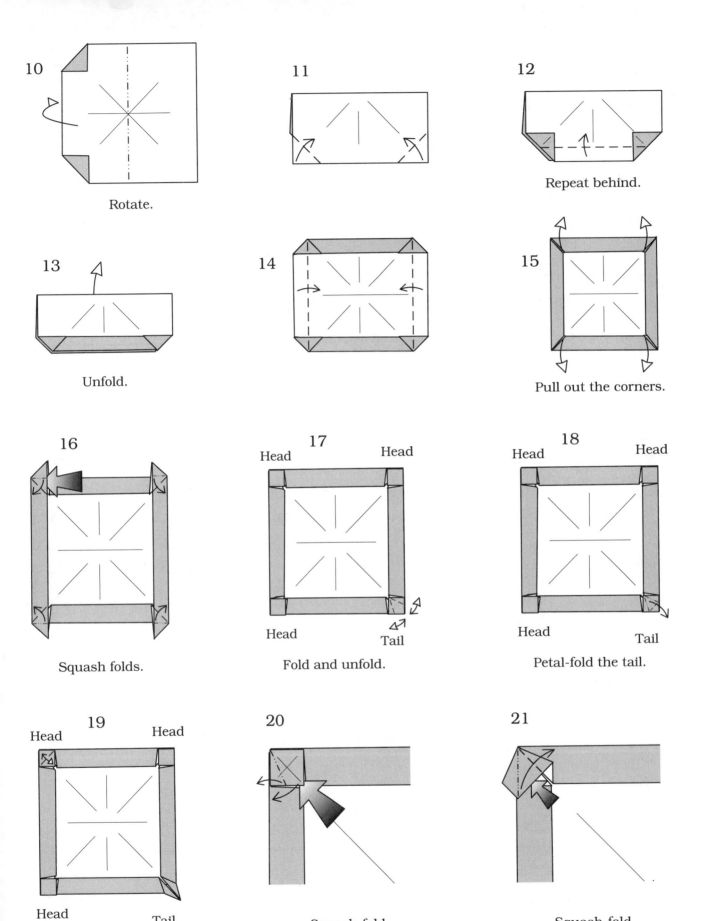

10

Rotate.

11

12

Repeat behind.

13

Unfold.

14

15

Pull out the corners.

16

Squash folds.

17

Head   Head

Head   Tail

Fold and unfold.

18

Head   Head

Head   Tail

Petal-fold the tail.

19

Head   Head

Head   Tail

Fold and unfold.

20

Squash-fold.

21

Squash-fold.

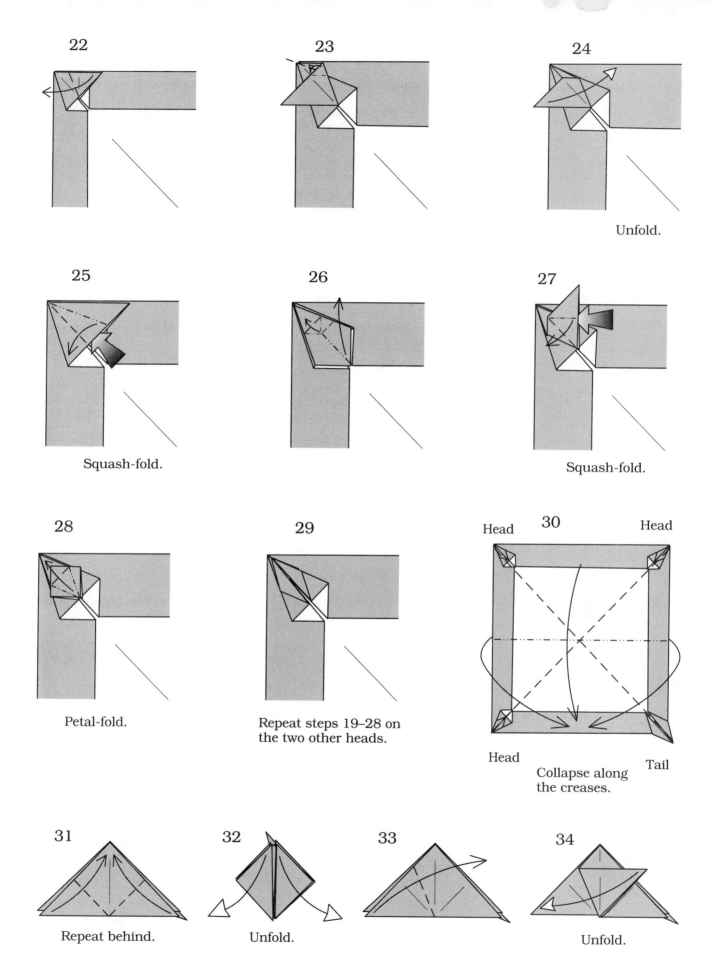

22

23

24

Unfold.

25

Squash-fold.

26

27

Squash-fold.

28

Petal-fold.

29

Repeat steps 19–28 on the two other heads.

30

Head   Head

Head   Tail

Collapse along the creases.

31

Repeat behind.

32

Unfold.

33

34

Unfold.

Three-Headed Dragon 113

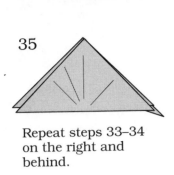

35

Repeat steps 33–34
on the right and
behind.

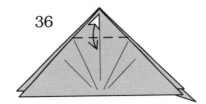

36

Fold down
and unfold.

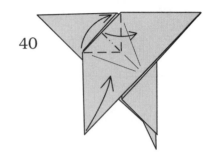

37

Fold and unfold,
repeat behind.

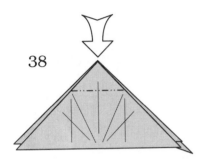

38

Begin the sink fold.

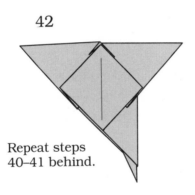

39

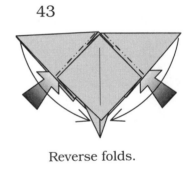

40

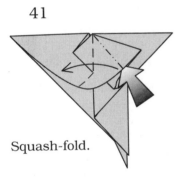

41

Squash-fold.

42

Repeat steps
40–41 behind.

43

Reverse folds.

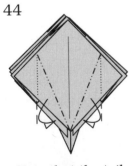

44

Note that the tail
is in the back.

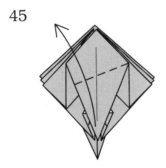

45

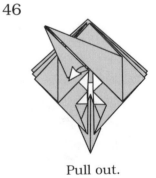

46

Pull out.

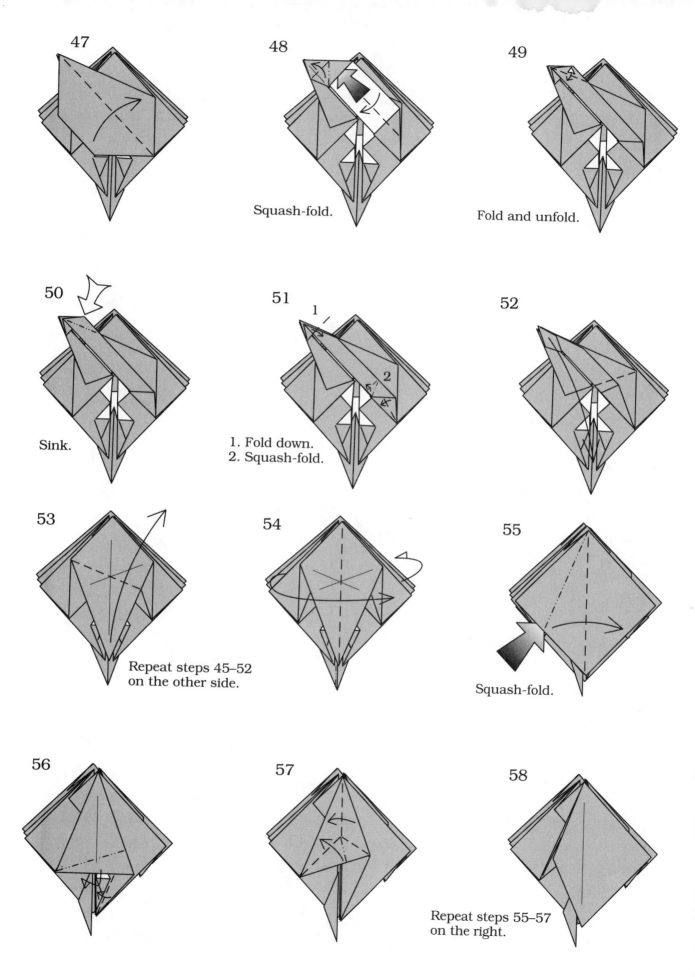

47

48

Squash-fold.

49

Fold and unfold.

50

Sink.

51

1. Fold down.
2. Squash-fold.

52

53

Repeat steps 45–52
on the other side.

54

55

Squash-fold.

56

57

58

Repeat steps 55–57
on the right.

Three-Headed Dragon 115

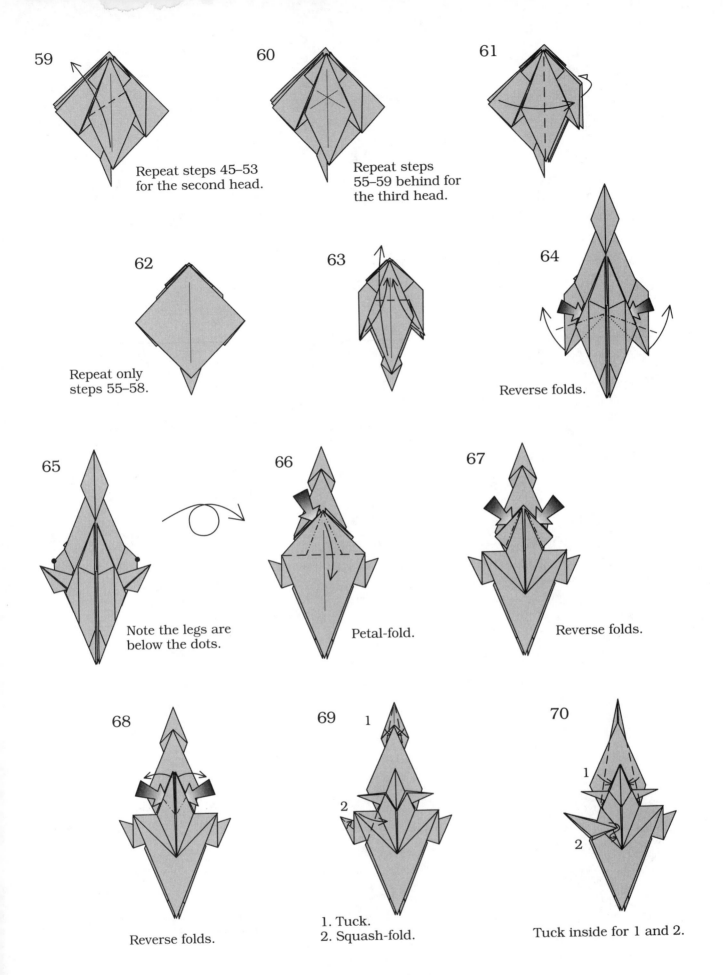

59

Repeat steps 45–53 for the second head.

60

Repeat steps 55–59 behind for the third head.

61

62

Repeat only steps 55–58.

63

64

Reverse folds.

65

Note the legs are below the dots.

66

Petal-fold.

67

Reverse folds.

68

Reverse folds.

69

1
2

1. Tuck.
2. Squash-fold.

70

1
2

Tuck inside for 1 and 2.

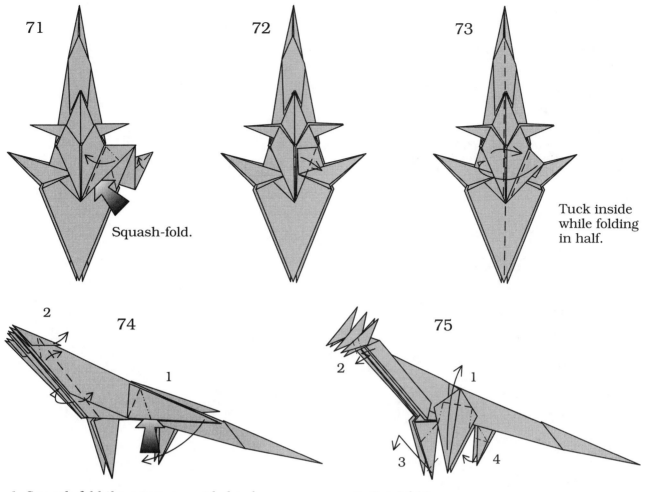

71

Squash-fold.

72

73

Tuck inside
while folding
in half.

74

2

1

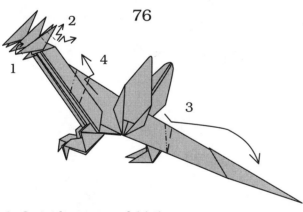

1. Squash-fold the wing, repeat behind.
2. Crimp-fold the neck, repeat for each neck.

75

2

1

3

4

1. Petal-fold.
2. Crimp-fold the mouth on the three heads.
3. Reverse folds.
4. Crimp-fold.
Repeat behind.

76

1

2

4

3

1. Outside-reverse-fold the nose.
2. Bend the horns.
Repeat 1 and 2 on the two other heads.
3. Crimp-fold and curl the tail.
4. Simple valley and mountain folds to
   separate the necks, repeat behind but
   not on the center neck.
You can modify the three-headed dragon
in many ways.

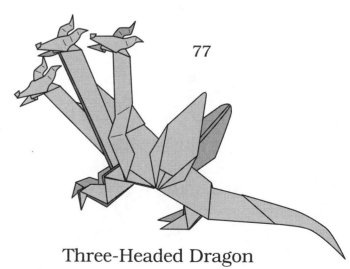

77

Three-Headed Dragon

Basic Folds

Rabbit Ear.

To fold a rabbit ear, one corner is folded in half and laid down to a side.

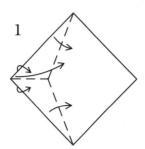

1

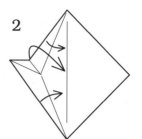

2

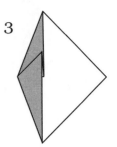

3

Fold a rabbit ear.

A three-dimensional intermediate step.

Double Rabbit Ear.

If you were to bend a straw you would be folding the double rabbit ear.

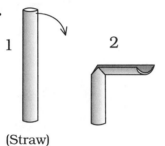

1   2

(Straw)

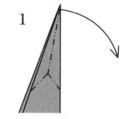

1

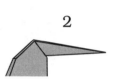

2

Make a double rabbit ear.

Squash Fold.

In a squash fold, some paper is opened and then made flat. The shaded arrow shows where to place your finger.

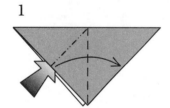

1

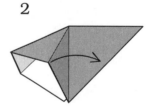

2

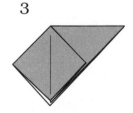

3

Squash-fold.

A three-dimensional intermediate step.

Petal Fold.

In a petal fold, one point is folded up while two opposite sides meet each other.

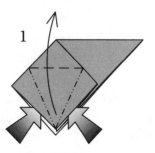

1

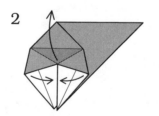

2

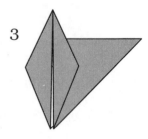

3

Petal-fold.

A three-dimensional intermediate step.

Inside Reverse Fold.

In an inside reverse fold, some paper is folded between layers. Here are two examples.

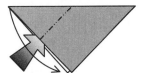

Reverse-fold.

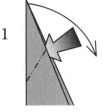

Reverse-fold.

Outside Reverse Fold.

Much of the paper must be unfolded to make an outside reverse fold.

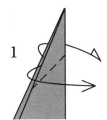

Outside-reverse-fold.

Crimp Fold.

A crimp fold is a combination of two reverse folds.

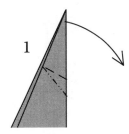
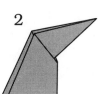

Crimp-fold.

Sink Fold.

In a sink fold, some of the paper without edges is folded inside. To do this fold, much of the model must be unfolded.

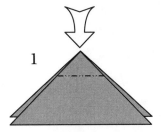
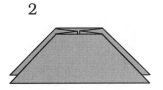

Sink.

Spread Squash Fold.

A cross between a squash fold and sink fold, some paper in the center is spread apart and then made flat.

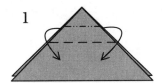
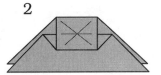

Spread-squash-fold.

Thou hast seen
What lies inside
Close the door
Let them abide